THE WILD CHEF

FIELD & STREAM

THE WILD CHEF

JONATHAN MILES

weldon**owen**

FALL 14

Venison Tenderloin | Thanksgiving Wild Turkey | Venison Sausage, Apple & Cranberry Dressing | Hungarian Fisherman's Soup | Field Dressing & Aging Deer | Venison Shoulder Roast with Wild Mushrooms | Buttermilk-Poached Walleye | Dress Up Your Venison | Venison & Pumpkin Curry | Wild Boar Stew | Essential Kitchen Tools | Cider-Braised Rabbit | Salt-Crusted Fish | Butchering Deer | Venison-Stuffed Tamales | The Joy of Squirrels | Squirrel, Biscuits, & Gravy | Grill-Roasted Fish | Partridge Two Ways | Irish Angler's Pie | Venison Pierogi | Adventures in Venison | Grilled Marinated Venison Heart | Seared Venison Liver | Venison Steak & Kidney Empanadas | Braised Venison Tongue | Buttermilk-Fried Quail | Blackened Venison Steaks | Root Beer–Glazed Duck | Seared Pheasant Breasts

WINTER 70

Venison Backstrap with Red Pears | Wild Game Ravioli | Braised Rabbit with Rosemary | Field Dressing Small Game | Wild Game Mincemeat Cobbler | Roasted Grouse with Mushrooms & Bacon | Essential Salts | Duck Prosciutto | Elk & Toasted Chile Stew | Roasted Goose with Cranberry, Oyster & Chestnut Stuffing | Citrus-Glazed Fish | Roasted Leg of Venison | Venison Osso Buco | Butchering Birds | Duck Salmi | Braised & Barbecued Venison Ribs | Venison Nachos | Goose Leg Sliders | Braised Squirrel | Moose Stew | Venison Cassoulet | History of Chili | Ultimate Camp Chili | Mary of Agreda's Chili | Christmas (Beer-Can) Goose | Stewed Duck with Apples & Turnips | Rabbit Sott'olio | Elk Carbonnade | Backcountry Paella | The Ice Fisherman's Breakfast

SPRING 126

Trout, Fiddlehead Ferns & Scrambled Eggs | Freezer-Raid Gumbo | Black Bear Empanadas | Little Fish, Big Flavor | Ultimate Fried Bream | Oat-Crusted Trout with Stovies | Prepping Your Catch | Pickled Pike | Wild-Game Banh Mi | Essential Knives | Wild Turkey Potpie | Deer Dogs with Pea Soup Sauce | Hawaiian Fish Jerky | Largemouth Bass Tacos | Wild Turkey Roulades | Morels: The Turkey Hunter's Mushroom | Turkey Soup with Morels | Braised Bear Shanks | Green Chile Venison Stew | Trout on a Nail | Wild Turkey Scallops | Fix the Perfect Shore Lunch | Panfish Chowder

SUMMER 172

Venison Sliders | The Lake Erie Monster | Essential Camp Kitchen Gear | Salmon Kebabs with Horseradish Butter | Grilled Venison Backstrap with Deer Rub | The Montauk Burger | Deckside Ceviche | Open Fire Cooking | Grilled Dove Pizza | Perfectly Grilled Whole Fish | Doves from Hell | The Willow Skillet | Trucker's Rice with Venison Jerky | Fried Crappie | Eat More Bass | Pan-Roasted Largemouth Bass | Wok-Steamed Whole Fish | The Ultimate Summer Gig | Cedar-Roasted Char | Whole Fried Catfish with Green Onions | Butter-Braised Fish | The Sweet Life

FOR
BARBARA MILES
WHO TAUGHT ME HOW TO COOK

AND IN MEMORY OF
RALPH A. MILES (1926–2007)
WHO TAUGHT ME HOW TO SHOOT

FOREWORD

Just like how the heat of a cast-iron skillet can turn a venison backstrap from perfectly seared to inedible if left on too long, so too can a wild game meal lose its flavor when reverence—no matter how deserved—is overdone.

That's why you don't often hear hunters talk about "locavores." Before these creatures started popping up everywhere in media—pontificating about locally sourced, humanely slaughtered, organic meat—there was hunting and fishing, and there were outdoorsmen. We've been doing this for years, and we know why it's important, so why make a big deal about it?

For one thing, I think that it is a big deal that sportsmen are getting some positive attention from many different areas of our culture. From television cooking shows to celebrity chefs to—yes—even well-intentioned but annoying hipsters who are taking up hunting, the more nonhunters who understand and respect our sports, the better for all of us.

A very practical reason this is a big deal are all the awesome ideas and techniques that modern chefs are bringing to wild game cooking. Jonathan Miles—sportsman, cook, writer, and world-class eater—is *Field & Stream's* Wild Chef and the ideal guide to the evolving world of fish and game cooking. He shares these trends and techniques in the pages that follow, based on hundreds of recipes and meals shared with professional chefs and deeply experienced wild game cooking experts.

The professionals often speak about getting the best possible ingredient and then preparing it in a way that respects and honors its natural flavor. For a hunter like me, words like best, respect, and honor sound like the only way to think about the deeply flavorful meat of the bull elk in my freezer. Unfortunately this is where sportsmen sometimes get lost. You can't cook game the way you cook domestic animals, and if you're not careful you can end up with a dried-out piece of meat that people will call "gamey." Or worse, you can drown all of that wild flavor under the industrial ooze of a can of cream-of-mushroom soup. This book can help make sure you never do that again.

While some recipes in this book are ambitious and designed for special occasions, many others aren't hard and are perfect for everyday use. For outdoorsmen, wild fish and game is not a rare treat—it's what's for dinner. It's the ground meat in our spaghetti sauce, the fried fillet on our tacos. But food is one of those areas in life that blend the high and low, the celebratory and mundane. It is the basic necessity we stuff in our faces on the drive to work and it is the family Thanksgiving holiday and our anniversary dinner. Daily sustenance or special celebration, it's all in this book.

A meal of fish or game can be both, but no matter how it's consumed it brings with it some extra flavor. For the sportsmen, it can conjure a morning high on the mountaintop or dusk spent in the stillness of a lake. It brings with it the hard, cold power of a surging fish, the instinct and beauty of a migrating mallard, and the wisdom and wildness of whitetail.

If that doesn't deserve our respect, nothing does.

ANTHONY LICATA
EDITOR-IN-CHIEF
FIELD & STREAM

INTRODUCTION

I learned *how* to eat the same way everyone else does: as a baby, slurping mush from a spoon. About ten years later, however, I learned what it *meant* to eat. That's when I shot a dove off a tree in my neighbor's backyard with a .177-caliber Crosman air rifle. Until that moment I'd never shot anything livelier than a Coke can; sobbing with panic and guilt, I leapt the wall into my neighbor's yard to fetch the downed bird, convinced I'd just committed some kind of grievous sin. Back then, children like me were called "latchkey kids," meaning that the hours between the school dismissal and my parents' return from work were mine and mine alone— so I could've buried the dead bird or otherwise hidden it somewhere. But that struck me as adding yet another layer of sin: wasting a life after taking it. The moral course, I somehow knew, was to eat the dove.

So I did. Not elegantly, of course. I breasted out the bird—even for an 11-year-old boy, it's not hard to find the meat on a dove—and cooked the meat the only way I knew how to cook anything: by broiling it atop a Triscuit cracker, the same way I cooked myself Triscuit pizzas after school. And though hot tears of confused shame still came streaming down my face as I ate it, with each bite something else occurred to me—something lasting and profound. This was what I did every day when I ate meat, I realized: I nurtured my own life via the death of another life. Nature's cruel and beautiful order became clearer and clearer to me with every bite, and it hit me, even then, that this was the first honest meal I'd ever eaten. Years later, I'd come to understand that this was what the Spanish philosopher José Ortega y Gasset had in mind when he called man a fugitive from nature. To disregard the source of our meat—to ignore the deaths that sustain our own lives—is to deny our predatory essence, to hide from the reality of biology. To hunt is to own up to that essence, and to face the full scope of our appetites.

That was a ferociously big realization for a kid, of course. But it wasn't the only one: I couldn't help noting that dove meat, which was unlike anything I'd ever tasted before, was flat-out delicious.

With fewer tears and more powerful guns, I've been recreating that moment for more than thirty years—with more doves, of course, and with squirrels and ducks and quail and wild turkeys and boar and deer. And with rod and reel, too, guiding fish out of the water and into the skillet. Though I enjoy all the fringe benefits of hunting and angling—the boozy camaraderie of camp, the way the toxic pressures of life seep out of you in a treestand, the adrenaline rush of a fish on the line or of your prey edging into view—my primary interest has always been culinary. I take to the woods and water to feed an old and particular hunger: a hunger for honest meat, for meat with that sublime range of flavors that only the wild provides, and for that sharp awareness of the meaning of eating that so stung me as a child—and exhilarated me, too.

In the past decade or so we've witnessed a very welcome revolution in the way Americans think about their food. Free range is the ideal. Organic, too. Ditto for local. At the risk of self-satisfied glibness, those of us who hunt and fish can boast that we've been eating free-range, organic, and local since the very beginning. That we haven't always cooked it well, however, will come as no surprise to anyone whose taste buds were scarred by Grandpa's overcooked venison steaks, or by those poor quail of his, drowned in a gray slurry of cream-of-mushroom soup. To be fair to Grandpa, however, we should cite a couple of the cultural headwinds he faced—for one thing, subtle cookery tended to be Grandma's forte, not his. Then there's the fact that for decades, the aesthetic goal of wild game cookery was to mask its woodsy flavors, not highlight them. Yet the revolution in American eating has also been a revolution in American cooking, and hunters and anglers who once killed their prey twice—once in the field, then again in the kitchen—have enthusiastically embraced the culinary side of their pursuits.

We at *Field & Stream* launched the "Wild Chef" column in 2004 to help cultivate and encourage this revival in game and fish cookery, and to provide our readers with opportunities for adventure even after the guns and tackle boxes have been packed away. A giant thicket of antlers is no longer the sole symbol of a successful deer hunt; a perfectly-cooked backstrap, maybe pan-roasted with red pears and served with pickled golden raisins (see page 73 for the recipe), has, for many of us, become the ultimate trophy. Because while hunting and fishing are often called sports, they are, at heart, a kind of foraging—a prelude to eating. I'm fond of what the late Havilah Babcock wrote in *Field & Stream* back in 1964: "I still like to bring home something to grace the dinner table when I go hunting and fishing, and I can imagine no finer reason for going. The world was made to be lived in as well as looked at, and nature's supermarket is well stocked if you don't mind its self-service feature." And I'm fonder still of what George Perry, the Georgia angler who still holds the world record for the 22-lb., 4-oz. largemouth bass he caught in 1932, once said about that day of historic fishing: "We were out to catch dinner."

JONATHAN MILES

FALL

For the hunter, fall begins much earlier than the calendar says it does. For some, it starts in a millet or sunflower field awash in the slanted golden light of late summer, the hunters snapping to their feet to shoot as doves come flitting through the sky like comets.

For others, fall begins more subtly, when the landscape telegraphs a faint signal—one's breath made visible by an evening wind sweeping down from the north; the distant honking of geese getting an early start on their V-shaped odyssey; or merely the peripheral sight of a single leaf curling softly earthward—that swells the heart with its familiar expectation, and sends the hunter to his guns for cleaning and oiling and for an ancient variety of daydreaming.

As the Harvest Moon gives way to the Hunter's Moon, these expectations are carried into the woods for fulfillment: the rabbit and squirrel hunters stalking their way along a ridge, the dry coiled leaves underfoot whispering to their boots; the waterfowl hunters sunk into their blinds, eyes trained on the violet clouds of dawn; and the deer hunters perched like statuary in a treestand, half-breathing in anticipation.

For hunters and cooks alike, this is the year's pinnacle—the season of bounty, the abundance of the garden melding with the abundance of wild flavor from what the hunter brings from the woods. "It is not my home," the narrator of William Faulkner's epilogue to the stories in *Big Woods* says of his residence in town (his home, by most measures) which he escapes every autumn to go hunting in the cypress-thick bottomlands. "It is merely the way station," he explains, "in which I pass the time waiting for November again."

VENISON TENDERLOIN WITH SAGE, PUMPKIN & PRUNES

Elements like pumpkins and prunes make this dish—from Terrance Brennan of New York's Picholine—a perfect fall meal, and its bright, rich colors on the plate lend it some stunning visual appeal. Either tenderloin or backstrap will work for this dish.

Kosher salt and freshly ground black pepper

½ teaspoon ground allspice

¼ teaspoon ground star anise

¼ teaspoon cinnamon

6 tablespoons (3 fl oz/90 ml) canola oil

4 venison tenderloins, 6–7 oz (185–220 g) each

Packed ¼ cup (1½ oz/45 g) prunes, finely chopped

2 tablespoons Armagnac or cognac (optional)

12 tablespoons (1½ sticks/6 oz/185 g) unsalted butter, softened at room temperature, cut into tablespoon-size pieces

2 cups (13 oz/410 g) peeled and finely diced cheese pumpkin or other baking pumpkin

10 fresh sage leaves, minced

In a bowl, stir together 1½ teaspoons salt, ½ teaspoon pepper, the allspice, the star anise, and the cinnamon. Whisk in 2 tablespoons of the oil. Rub this mixture onto both sides of each venison loin.

Put the prunes in a bowl. If using Armagnac, pour it over prunes and set them aside to soak.

In a 10-inch (25-cm) sauté pan over medium heat, heat 2 tablespoons of the remaining oil and 2 tablespoons of the butter. Add the pumpkin and cook, tossing and stirring every few minutes, until lightly caramelized on all sides, 15–18 minutes. Toss in the prunes. Remove the pan from the heat and season generously with salt and pepper.

Preheat the oven to 350°F (180°C). Put 2 tablespoons each of the remaining oil and butter in a 12-inch (30-cm) ovenproof sauté pan over medium-high heat. When butter starts to sizzle and foam, add the venison loins and sear for 1 minute. Turn them over and transfer the pan to the oven. Roast until an instant-read thermometer inserted in the center of a loin reads 120°F (49°C) for rare. Remove the pan from the oven and transfer the venison to a board. Let rest 3–4 minutes.

Meanwhile, heat a sauté pan over medium-high heat. Add the remaining butter and cook it until it melts and turns brown, approximately 1 minute. Remove the pan from the heat and stir in the sage leaves. When the sage leaves get crispy, scoop them out and set aside.

Divide the pumpkin and prunes evenly among dinner plates. Top each portion with a venison loin, a drizzle of brown butter, and crisped sage.

▶ **NEXT-DAY DISH** Odds are decent that you'll finish every last bite of venison here, but if there is any left over, then you have the star ingredient for a killer sandwich. Smear each half of a crusty baguette with mayonnaise, add the venison, cilantro, and a drizzle of Sriracha, and enjoy. —C.K.

THANKSGIVING WILD TURKEY

For many hunter-cooks, Thanksgiving is a holiday of pride—the one day a year their field and kitchen prowess are put on display for family and friends. This recipe ensures that full measure of pride.

¾ lb (375 g) fatback, salted pork, or bacon*, minced

1 wild turkey, 11–13 lb (5.5–6.5 kg)

Coarse salt and freshly ground black pepper

1 yellow onion, minced

3 ribs celery, minced

4 cloves garlic, minced

4 cups (8 oz/250 g) toasted diced bread

1 cup (8 fl oz/250 ml) chicken stock

6 sprigs sage, minced

2 sprigs rosemary, minced

8 sprigs Italian parsley, minced

*Have your butcher slice this thinly into sheets resembling slices of American cheese.

Preheat the oven to 350°F (180°C). Render half of the fatback slowly in a heavy-bottom sauté pan. Reserve and keep warm.

Dry the turkey very well with paper towels. Using a brush, coat the exterior with some of the warm minced fatback and season well with salt and pepper inside and out.

Heat up the remaining minced fatback on medium. Add the onion and season with salt and pepper. Cook for 5 minutes, stirring occasionally, then add the celery and cook for 5 minutes more. Add the garlic and cook for 1 minute. Remove from the heat and add the toasted bread. Moisten with stock and add the minced herbs. Taste the bread cubes and add more broth and herbs as needed—they should be moist and tasty. Gently fill the cavity of the turkey with this mixture, and cover the breast with the remaining slices of fatback.

Place the turkey, breast side up, in a heavy roasting pan and put it in the oven. Roast for 1 hour. Remove the fatback, raise the oven temperature to 375°F (190°C), and continue roasting for 1 hour to brown the breast. Remove the turkey as soon as it registers 160°F (71°C) on an instant-read thermometer inserted into the thickest part of the thigh, away from the bone.

Let the turkey rest for at least 20–30 minutes before carving it across the grain with a sharp knife. —C.K.

HOW TO CARVE A THANKSGIVING GOBBLER

There may be other deeds more laden with American pomp than carving a Thanksgiving turkey—folding the Stars and Stripes comes to mind—but there aren't many that train so keen a spotlight on a single moment, a single person, a single act with a knife in hand. The bird has been in the oven long enough to send its aroma wafting through the house, and now the gathered clan sits at the table, gawking at all the wedding china and silver that has emerged from the attic on a schedule similar to that of Halley's comet. All eyes turn to the turkey. Don't screw this up.

By now you should have paved the way for a civil service. Go ahead and decide which kids get the drumsticks before you say grace—no use ruining the meal with a fistfight right out of the gate. Let folks know they shouldn't eat till Grandma first lifts her fork. No cursing. No ketchup bottles on the table. And honestly, it's a celebration, so if little Johnny wants to slip a Whoopee Cushion under Grandpap's seat, where's the harm?

But know this: The very act of carving a turkey—especially a wild turkey—changes the game at the table. It's the moment when something—the essence of which is undeniably, unabashedly wild—transfigures into the building block of civilization: human food. Each of us closes that circle with a fork.

It's a metamorphosis worthy of a moment's contemplation, at the least, and worthy of the giving of thanks. And for the sake of Ben Franklin and all things pure and true, forego any blade that comes with a power cord sticking out of the handle. —T.E.N.

VENISON SAUSAGE, APPLE & CRANBERRY DRESSING

Since stuffing a turkey draws juices out of the bird and into the stuffing, lean wild turkeys can benefit from cooking a dressing alongside, instead. Here's a beautifully autumnal option that will make for an excellent sandwich component.

SERVES 4

Kosher salt and freshly ground black pepper

6 tablespoons (3 oz/90 g) butter plus more for greasing

2 cups (12 oz/375 g) finely chopped yellow onion

¾ cup (3 oz/90 g) chopped celery

¼ cup (3½ oz/105 g) chopped green bell pepper

1 lb (500 g) smoked venison sausage, diced

8 cups (16 oz/500 g) crusty, good-quality bread, cut into ½-inch (12-mm) cubes and toasted in the oven

1 cup (4 oz/125 g) peeled and diced Granny Smith apples

¾ cup (3 oz/90 g) dried cranberries

½ cup (¾ oz/20 g) chopped Italian parsley

1½ tablespoons chopped fresh sage, or 2 teaspoons dried sage

¾ cup (6 fl oz/180 ml) chicken stock

Preheat the oven to 325°F (165°C) and grease a casserole dish with butter. In a large skillet, melt 6 tablespoons of butter over medium-high heat. Sauté the onion, celery, and bell pepper until the onion is translucent. Add the sausage and sauté for another 4 minutes. Put the mixture in a bowl and add all the remaining ingredients except for the stock. Add the stock little by little until the dressing is moist; you want it loose, not clumpy. Transfer the dressing to the prepared casserole dish and cover with foil or a lid.

When your turkey has about 1½ hours left to go, place the dressing alongside it in the oven. Cook the dressing covered for 1 hour and 15 minutes, then remove the cover and cook until the top is crisp and lightly browned, another 15 minutes or so.

Serve alongside the turkey.

HUNGARIAN FISHERMAN'S SOUP

For centuries, fishermen along the Danube and Tisza Rivers in Hungary have added an iron kettle to their fishing gear. The reason? To make *halászlé*, or fisherman's soup, a spicy red stew that's often cooked streamside over a campfire. Variations are infinite, but the essential components are whole freshwater fish and high-quality Hungarian paprika.

SERVES 4

About 3 lb (1.5 kg) whole freshwater fish

1 large onion, roughly chopped

2 green bell peppers, roughly chopped

1 tomato, roughly chopped

2 bay leaves

2 tablespoons or more Hungarian paprika (hot, sweet, or a combination)

Salt and freshly ground black pepper

¼ cup (⅓ oz/10 g) chopped fresh Italian parsley

½ cup (4 oz/125 g) sour cream (optional)

2 banana peppers, sliced (optional)

Gut and clean the fish, separating the fillets but reserving the heads and other scraps. Slice the fillets into 2-inch (5-cm) pieces, rinse, and refrigerate until ready to use. Add the scraps—heads, tails, bones, trimmings—to a Dutch oven or large pot. Add the onion, peppers, tomato, bay leaves, and paprika along, with 2 quarts (2 l) cold water, and bring to a simmer over medium heat. Reduce the heat and simmer, uncovered, for 35 minutes.

Strain the liquid into another pot through a fine-mesh sieve. Press on the solids to extract all the flavor, then discard. Add salt and pepper to taste. The broth should have a good kick from the paprika—feel free to add more if necessary.

Return the broth to a simmer, and add the reserved fillet pieces. Simmer gently, without stirring, for a few minutes—just enough to almost cook the fish through, since it will continue cooking off the heat. Add the parsley, stirring very gently so as not to break up the fish.

▶ **SERVING TIP** Transfer the fish pieces with a slotted spoon and divide among 4 bowls. Ladle the liquid into the bowls and top with a dollop of sour cream and a few slices of banana peppers, if using.

WHY THE WOODEN SPOON IS THE PERFECT TOOL

When it comes to kitchen utensils, particularly the almighty spoon—that all-purpose tool that serves, stirs, scrapes, and scoops—you typically have three choices: Metal, plastic, and wood.

I choose wood. Always.

You'd think I'd be opposed to wooden spoons, as they were my mother's primary form of discipline for my siblings and me when we were growing up. We'd often get a whack on the bottom when we deserved it. Still, my utensil jar today is filled with wooden spoons, and they remain my favorite, so maybe I picked up a predilection for them through rear-end osmosis.

Or maybe I like wood best because it's the most versatile of kitchen tools. A wooden spoon can jump from cast iron to nonstick to stainless pans without any chance of scratching. A wooden spoon doesn't change the taste of acidic foods, such as tomato sauce, the way metal might. A wooden spoon won't melt or become too hot to handle if you leave it in the pot. Best of all, a wooden spoon feels damn good in the hand—like it belongs there.

I've heard some people complain that wooden spoons are tougher to clean than plastic or metal. True, there might be some staining with use, but only if you don't clean them like you should. And you should clean and take care of them, because these are our tools we're talking about. If you can't or won't take care of your tools, well, then you deserve a lot worse than a whack on the behind from Mom.
—D.D.

FIELD DRESSING & AGING DEER

So, you've shot a deer. Good for you. No matter if it's your first or fiftieth, this is a moment to savor and preserve. It's also the moment at which you need to accept the responsibility that comes with killing an animal. Before you even start to think of new recipes or imagine how the antlers might look on your wall, there's work to be done. How your venison tastes is directly linked to two factors. The first is field dressing, and it's called that for a reason—it needs to be done quickly, in the field. So roll up your sleeves, sharpen your knife, and get going. The second factor is aging. As much as you'll want to come home and celebrate the hunt with fresh backstrap steaks, you must practice patience. The deer needs to hang in a cool place—for as long as two weeks—for the meat to reach its tender peak. Of course, you won't have to wait that long for your first meal— assuming you made a clean shot, you'll have the heart and liver, which are both delicious and should be enjoyed sooner rather than later. Now, let's get to work.

DRESS ACCORDINGLY

1 Horse the deer over on its back. Its head should be uphill from its hindquarters. Grab a handful of belly skin, nick it with your knife, and slide the blade in, edge upward, not letting the point ride down into the body cavity. Taking utmost care not to puncture the innards, slit the belly skin from crotch to sternum.

2 When the body cavity is open, reach inside and haul everything out, cutting carefully to free stuff where necessary. If you like to eat the heart and liver, set them aside.

3 Reach up into the throat and cut out the windpipe. Cut around the anus, free the lower intestine, and remove it. Get behind the deer and lift it as though you were doing a Heimlich maneuver; let all the blood run out of the body cavity. If there's snow, shovel it into the cavity and let it soak up the blood.

4 If you're ready to drag, tie the critter's forelegs alongside its head and start pulling. If you have to go for help, prop open the body cavity with a stick so that heat can escape. That's all there is to it. —D.E.P.

DEER HEART APPETIZERS

Any first deer—first of your life, first of the season, first of the day—is a reason to celebrate. No need to go crazy with the mysticism, but the heart is a meaningful way to honor the seriousness of taking a life to give life.

Slice the heart into ⅜-inch-thick slices. Dredge in an egg bath, then white flour, then back in the egg bath, and next through saltine cracker crumbs. Fry in bacon grease or vegetable oil until golden brown. Don't overcook. Cut into quarter-size pieces, and serve with hot sauce between hands of poker. —T.E.N.

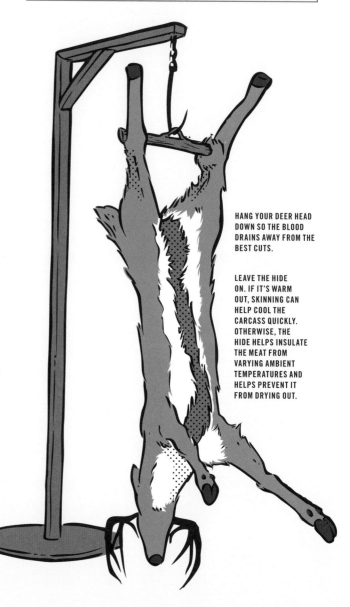

HANG YOUR DEER HEAD DOWN SO THE BLOOD DRAINS AWAY FROM THE BEST CUTS.

LEAVE THE HIDE ON. IF IT'S WARM OUT, SKINNING CAN HELP COOL THE CARCASS QUICKLY. OTHERWISE, THE HIDE HELPS INSULATE THE MEAT FROM VARYING AMBIENT TEMPERATURES AND HELPS PREVENT IT FROM DRYING OUT.

HANG TIMELINE

How long should you hang your deer? The answer: Until the meat is tender—and that depends on your deer. The purpose of aging an animal is to allow naturally-occurring enzymes enough time to break down collagen—the fibrous connective tissue that binds muscle cells together and makes meat tough. Generally, the older the deer, the more collagen it has, and the longer this takes. Here's an aging timeline to follow for your next deer.

DAY 1

If you butcher your deer today, don't freeze it. Rigor mortis sets in after death, lasting 12–24 hours, and will contract and stiffen muscle tissue. Freezing at this point results in thaw rigor, a.k.a. "shoe leather."

TIP If temps are high, try wet-aging: Cool the carcass with ice for 12 hours. When butchering, keep whole muscles intact. Drain off any blood, pat dry and vacuum-seal the cuts, and let age in the fridge for a week.

DAYS 2–4

If you shot a yearling, process it now. These deer are tender and don't need as much hang time. Remove the skin and shorten the hang time for other deer if temps are on the high side, as this makes both collagen breakdown and bacterial growth happen faster.

TIP You can process the cuts you plan to make into sausage or burger shortly after rigor mortis—even with older deer—as grinding effectively tenderizes the meat.

DAYS 5–8

This is the hang time many hunters prefer under ideal conditions: 34–37°F (1–3°C). It's just about right for any middle-aged deer (2½–3½ years old) and perfectly adequate for many older deer.

TIP If temperatures temporarily spike, put a bag of ice in the chest cavity and wrap the carcass in a blanket or old sleeping bag to keep the cold in.

DAYS 9–13

The older your deer, the more connective tissue in its muscles and the more benefit from extra days on the meat pole. If conditions are consistently good and you can keep a close eye on the meat, 2 weeks is not too long to hang an old buck.

TIP Ambient temperatures matter, of course, but what counts most is the internal temperature of the meat. Use a meat thermometer to regularly take your deer's temp.

DAY 14

The rate at which meat is tenderized as a result of aging falls off sharply after 14 days. In other words, time to wrap it up.

TIP Like high temperatures, high humidity and moisture can promote bacteria growth, so you should avoid getting the carcass wet. If you don't have a dry place to store it, don't age it this long. —D.H.

TEACH A YOUNG BLOOD

Field dressing becomes an entirely new animal when your child is there with you to watch—particularly if it's for the first time. Introducing a young hunter to the labor of turning what was once a living, breathing creature into bundles of neatly labeled meat demands thought and care. Here are some rules to help.

DON'T MAKE A FUSS Teach your kid that what happens after the rifle shot is just another part of the deal. Gutting and skinning an animal is nothing to dread. It's as much a part of hunting as lacing your boots, so treat it that way.

DON'T PUSH IT, EITHER On the other hand, recognize that the notion of removing the organs and severing the joints from an animal with a saw is not exactly a stroll through Candy Land. Go easy. You're not out to prove a point or toughen up a soft kid. Also, if you think you might have crippled an animal, get your child out of the picture immediately.

BE METHODICAL Talk through every step, pointing out the animal's body structures. And give your child a job. Even if he's too young to handle a knife, he can hold a leg while you open up the body cavity, or pull back the rib cage as you remove the lungs and heart.

SEE IT THROUGH The learning experience doesn't need to end with field dressing. Involve your child in butchering, freezing, and other preparation tasks. If a pile of bloody meat gives your kid pause, then get him working on something else. Ask for help running the vacuum sealer, turning the grinder handle, or loading up the freezer. Help your child understand that a large part of killing an animal is devoted to sustaining another life—his own. —T.E.N.

VENISON SHOULDER ROAST WITH WILD MUSHROOMS

You'll need an entire venison shoulder for this dish, which comes from Chef John Besh of Restaurant August in New Orleans. He prefers the tougher cuts, like the shoulder, because they have more flavor—he even goes out of his way to rescue them from friends who only want to grind them for sausage. The accompanying turnip purée is one of the best things you'll try all year. As for the venison, you may never use the shoulder for sausage again.

SERVES 6

VENISON

1 shoulder of venison

Salt and freshly ground black pepper

¼ cup (2 fl oz/60 ml) bacon drippings

2 yellow onions, diced

1 carrot, peeled and diced

1 rib celery, diced

¼ cup (1½ oz/45 g) all-purpose flour

2 garlic cloves, crushed

1 cup (6 oz/185 g) canned diced tomatoes

2 apples, any type, cored and diced

2 oz (60 g) dried porcini or chanterelle mushrooms

2 cups (16 fl oz/500 ml) beef broth

1 cup (8 fl oz/250 ml) apple juice

1 cup (8 fl oz/250 ml) red wine

1 sprig fresh thyme or 1 teaspoon dried

1 sprig rosemary

2 bay leaves

1 dash sugar

TURNIP PURÉE

1 lb (500 g) turnips, peeled and diced

½ lb (250 g) potatoes, peeled and diced

½ lb (2 sticks/250 g) unsalted butter, diced

Salt

MAKE THE VENISON Season the venison shoulder with salt and pepper. In a large pot or Dutch oven over high heat, heat the bacon drippings, then brown the venison on both sides.

Remove the venison, then add the onions, carrot, and celery. Reduce the heat to medium and stir, cooking until the vegetables have become mahogany in color. Then stir in the flour. When the flour has been well incorporated, add the garlic, tomatoes, apples, and dried mushrooms.

Let the mixture come to a boil before slowly stirring in the beef broth, apple juice, and red wine. Raise the heat to high and bring to a boil again. Add the thyme, rosemary, bay leaves, sugar, and venison shoulder.

Reduce the heat to a low simmer, and cover the pot. Cook until the meat begins to pull easily from the bone with a fork, about 2 hours. Taste the sauce and season with salt and pepper.

Remove from the heat. Take out the venison shoulder and carefully pull the meat from the bone. Return meat to the cooking liquid and keep warm until ready to serve.

MAKE THE TURNIP PURÉE Put the turnips and potatoes in a pot and fill with enough water to cover the vegetables. Cover with a lid and bring to a boil over high heat. Reduce the heat to low and cook until the turnips are tender, about 20 minutes.

Drain the vegetables and transfer to a food-processor bowl. Add the butter and purée the mixture. Do not overprocess. Taste and season with salt. To serve, place a large scoop of turnip purée on a plate, and top with a generous spoonful of the venison shoulder and sauce.

▶ **DRINK PAIRING** Juniper is a traditional flavoring for venison, and the central flavoring for gin. Turn genever, a Dutch-style gin with robust character, into a Martinez: 2 oz sweet vermouth, 1 oz genever, and a dash each of maraschino liqueur and bitters. —C.K.

BUTTERMILK-POACHED WALLEYE

Poaching fish in buttermilk—a technique pioneered by New York superchef Jean-Georges Vongerichten—yields the familiar melt-away texture and pure flavor, but with a more sinful richness—and a poaching liquid you'll want to lap up with a spoon. I like walleye best for this, but any fish will be splendid this way—especially trout.

SERVES 4

1 tablespoon plus 4 tablespoons (2 oz/60 g) butter

2 slices bacon, preferably thick-cut, diced

2 bunches (1½ lb/750 g) mustard greens, stems and center ribs discarded and leaves halved

Salt and freshly ground black pepper

Four 6-oz (185-g) fillets of trout, walleye, pike, or other fish

3 cups (24 fl oz/750 ml) buttermilk

1 sprig fresh tarragon

Juice of 1 lemon

1 tablespoon fresh chives, finely chopped

Melt 1 tablespoon of the butter in a large sauté pan over medium-high heat. Add the bacon and cook until almost crisp. Add the greens and toss until they begin to wilt. Add about ½ cup (4 fl oz/125 ml) water and cook, covered, but stirring occasionally, for 5 minutes. Remove the lid and continue to cook until the greens are just tender and most of the liquid has evaporated. Season and keep warm until ready to serve.

Season the fillets and place them in a single layer in a large sauté pan. Pour over the buttermilk, add the tarragon, and place over medium heat. When the liquid begins to simmer, cover and cook for 2 minutes. Gently roll the fillets over, and cook for another minute, until the fish is firm but not falling apart.

With a slotted spatula, remove the fillets to a plate; keep warm. Discard the tarragon sprig. Transfer the buttermilk, which will have separated, to a blender and add the remaining 4 tablespoons butter. Blend until the butter is smoothly incorporated and the buttermilk is no longer separated. Add lemon juice, salt, and pepper to taste.

Place the greens in a shallow bowl and top with fish. Pour some buttermilk over top. Sprinkle with the chives and serve.

HOW TO COOK (AND ENJOY) TRASH FISH

GAR BALLS Gar can be really tough to catch with a hook and line, but a 12-inch piece of frayed nylon rope attached to a large barrel swivel will entice topwater strikes and tangle in their teeth securely enough to land them. As for eating one of these monsters, you'll need tin snips to open a gar's hide, but the fish has backstraps (loins, basically) that are shrimp-like in texture. Chop the meat and mix it with mashed potatoes, chopped onion, eggs, parsley, and some Cajun seasoning. Roll the mixture into hush puppy–size balls and, you guessed it, fry them in oil. (It's important to note that gar eggs are incredibly toxic to humans. Release female gar and keep only the smaller males for the table.)

HICKORY SHAD Here's an old-school/new-school angle for an anadromous fish that can be caught along the Atlantic coast.

Old school: Smoke whole gutted fish in a standard smoker. Use a fork to strip flakes of flesh from the bones. Eat and enjoy.

New school: Mix smoked shad with garlic, salt, tarragon, and lemon juice. Spread on crackers. Again, eat and enjoy.

BOWFIN Call it what you like—grinnell, blackfish, cypress trout—but old-timers called the bowfin dinner. Fillet the fish with the skin on, turn the fish skin side down, and use a spoon to scrape flesh from in between the bones. Mix with green onions, mashed potatoes, bread crumbs, 1 beaten egg, and more Cajun seasoning. Pan-fry in shallow oil. —W.B. & T.E.N.

3 SAUCES TO DRESS UP YOUR VENISON

The reason so many hunters prize venison medallions? They're the tenderest cut, they cook up quickly, and they're infinitely versatile. Try any of these sauces to dress up your sautéed medallions for very different—yet equally delicious—effects.

THE CLASSIC: CUMBERLAND SAUCE

The British aristocracy, whatever their faults, really do know how to sauce game. This zesty fruit-based sauce also goes well with lamb and pork. First, remove the zest from 1 orange with a grater or zester, and reserve. Juice the orange, and combine the orange juice in a small saucepan with the juice of ½ lemon, 1 cup (8 fl oz/250 ml) ruby port, 2 tablespoons red currant jelly, and ¼ teaspoon ground ginger. Bring to a boil over medium heat, then reduce the heat to a simmer. Simmer until the wine has reduced and the mixture is glossy and syrupy and easily coats a spoon, about 10 minutes. Taste and season with salt and freshly ground black pepper. Cover to keep warm, and set aside until ready to serve.

THE SHOWSTOPPER: FLAMING GIN SAUCE

Dinner guests to impress? When in doubt, set something on fire. Preferably the sauce, not the kitchen. Here's the game plan: Crush 6 juniper berries with the flat side of a knife and put them in a small saucepan with ½ cup (4 fl oz/125 ml) red wine. Cook over medium heat until the wine reduces to a syrupy consistency. Add about 1 cup (8 fl oz/250 ml) venison stock, chicken stock, and/or pan juices, and continue to cook until the stock has reduced as well. Remove from the heat and reserve.

Melt 1 tablespoon butter in a sauté pan over medium-high heat and add 2 minced shallots. Cook until the shallots are soft and golden, about 2 minutes. To flame the sauce, carefully remove the pan from the heat and add ¼ cup (2 fl oz/60 ml) gin. To ignite it, you can either return the pan to the stove and tilt the pan to catch the flame (this works on gas stoves only), or light the mixture with a long-handled match. Stand back—the flames will be high. Once the flames have subsided, stir the mixture, and continue to cook until most of the gin has evaporated. Add the reserved wine-and-stock mixture, and cook until the mixture coats a spoon, about 10 minutes. Drain the sauce through a fine-mesh sieve to remove the shallots, season with salt and freshly ground black pepper to taste, and return the sauce to the saucepan to keep warm until ready to serve.

HOW TO MAKE VENISON STOCK

Think about all of the work it takes to get from deer to venison: You scout, hunt, and shoot the deer. Then you field dress, age, and butcher the deer. By the time you're finished, there's nothing left but sinew and bones. It's an amazing process, but it's not over yet. Toss the sinew, save the bones—venison makes excellent stock. Even better, it allows you to use more of the animal, and you'll elevate your cooking when you can prepare rice or soup with homemade stock. Follow these tips for great stock:

- Use leg bones or neck bones, as they often have stray bits of meat on them. Adding meat makes a richer stock. Even better, toss in a venison shank or two.

- Never let the stock boil—bring it to a bare simmer only. Boiling will cloud the color of your stock and can make it taste bitter.

- Simmer meat for at least 3 hours before adding vegetables. Meat and bones take longer to give up their flavor, while veggies need only 1 to 2 hours, tops.

- Strain your stock with a fine-mesh strainer or, better yet, one lined with cheesecloth.

- Only add salt after you've strained the stock. Adding it too soon can result in a stock that's too salty at the end. And we can't have you go through all that work—scout, hunt, shoot, field dress, age, butcher, toss, save, stew, and cook—and wind up with salty stock. —H.S.

THE CURVEBALL: GARLIC & CILANTRO MOJO SAUCE

Bring out your most flavorful olive oil for this aromatic Cuban-style sauce. It's very simple, so the ingredients have to be good. Take 1 bunch cilantro and trim away the thicker stems. Put the leaves in a blender with 4 roughly chopped garlic cloves and 1 teaspoon salt. Process the mixture while slowly and steadily pouring in ¾ cup (6 fl oz/180 ml) extra-virgin olive oil. If the mixture is too thick, add a few tablespoons of water and pulse to combine—the mixture should be thick, but still pourable. Season to taste with 1–2 teaspoons sherry vinegar, red wine vinegar, or lemon juice.

VENISON & PUMPKIN CURRY

In Jamaica, a vibrant, aromatic curry would sauce mutton or goat, but it's a perfect match for venison, too—especially the meat from an older, more strongly flavored animal that could benefit from slow tenderizing and a powerful blast of exotic flavor. Venison and pumpkin make a classic autumn pairing, but with the tropical flavorings and chile-fueled heat, you won't be feeling any chill. Serve with lots of rice.

SERVES 4

1 lb (500 g) venison, cut into 2-inch (5-cm) cubes

2 tablespoons curry powder

1 teaspoon ground allspice

1 teaspoon ground coriander seed

Salt and freshly ground black pepper

2 tablespoons vegetable oil

1 yellow onion, chopped

2 large tomatoes, peeled and seeded

1 tablespoon tomato paste

3 garlic cloves, minced

8 oz (250 g) diced pumpkin (or other winter squash)

1 habanero chile, seeded and diced (optional)

¾ cup (6 fl oz/180 ml) chicken stock

2 tablespoons chopped cilantro

Steamed white rice for serving

Put the cubed venison in a large bowl along with the curry powder, allspice, coriander, and generous doses of salt and pepper. Mix well to combine the spices and to coat the meat. Refrigerate, covered, for at least 1 hour (preferably longer).

Heat a large pot or Dutch oven over medium-high heat. Add the vegetable oil. When the oil is just beginning to smoke, add the venison and sear until well-browned on all sides, about 8 minutes.

Add the onion, tomatoes, and tomato paste, and continue to cook, stirring, until the onions are limp, about 4 minutes. Add the garlic and cook for another minute. Add the pumpkin, chile (if using), and chicken stock, and bring to a simmer. Reduce the heat to low and simmer gently until the meat is very tender, 2 hours or more. Stir in the cilantro, and serve with lots of rice.

Keep in mind that the shelf life for spices is about a year. Make sure your curry powder is fresh for best results.

THE BEAUTY OF A POST-KILL RITUAL

It's not my place at all to suggest that there's a right way or a wrong way when it comes to a hunter's ritual practices. If a post-kill ritual doesn't come naturally, it's as disrespectful to fake it as it is to not consider one in the first place. Post-kill rituals can take quite a long time to develop—years or decades—and it's possible that as we age and become more attuned to our own mortality, we gain a greater interest in such matters.

The first part of my ritual is easy; it's what our parents told us a long time ago—please and thank you. I say thank you—very quietly, under my breath really—to the mountain I'm on and to the animal. Then I set about cleaning the animal. It's often too far from a road or trail to drag, so I quarter it for packing out. I like to leave the meat on the bone for aging, but I make sure the carcass that remains—head, vertebrae, ribs, shins—is positioned on its side, with each part as it was in life.

Last, I place my brass bullet casing against the trunk of the tree where I was sitting and position a rock over it. It's unlikely that I'll ever be back to that tree—there's too much new country to hunt and too few years. But I like to think that someday, maybe a century or more from now, a hunter might be sitting against that same tree.

I like to imagine that such a hunter will stop to remember that each of us is part of an ancient equation and relationship, one worthy of respect for our quarry, the landscape we hunt, and for ourselves—the manner in which we pursue our desire and our meals. Life is a privilege; the moments are almost always washing past. —R.B.

WILD BOAR STEW WITH SALSA VERDE

This crowd-pleaser, shared by chef Thomas McNaughton of Central Kitchen in San Francisco, is an ideal supper to cook at hunting camp because it leaves you free to enjoy hunting, napping, or playing cards while the Dutch oven does the work. Of course, when it's time to eat, you still get to take all the credit.

SERVES 4

SALSA VERDE

1 bunch Italian parsley

½ bunch spearmint

1 bunch tarragon

1 cup (8 fl oz/250 ml) olive oil

½ clove garlic

4 anchovy fillets

2 teaspoons capers

1 tablespoon Meyer lemon zest*

Juice of ½ Meyer lemon

Salt and freshly ground black pepper

WILD BOAR STEW

1 lb (500 g) dried cannellini beans

3 tablespoons olive oil

1 yellow onion, cut into 2-inch
(5-cm) pieces

2 carrots, peeled and cut into
2-inch (5-cm) pieces

2 ribs celery, cut into 2-inch
(5-cm) pieces

1 clove garlic, roughly chopped

2 lb (1 kg) boar shoulder, cut into
2-inch (5-cm) cubes

2½ cups (16 fl oz/500 ml) chicken
stock, or as needed

½ lb (250 g) pumpkin, diced

2 heads radicchio, chopped

*If you can't get Meyer lemons, substitute a blend of lemon and orange zest and juice to approximate the milder flavor of this lemon variety. Or just go tart.

MAKE THE SALSA VERDE Pick all the herb leaves from their stems and cut into long, thin slices. With a mortar and pestle, crush the herbs in batches until a paste forms. Scrape the paste into a plastic bowl and cover with the olive oil. In the last batch, crush the garlic, anchovies, and capers. Combine all ingredients with the lemon zest and juice. Add salt and pepper to taste.

MAKE THE WILD BOAR STEW Rinse the beans and put them in a large pot with water to cover generously. Soak for at least 4 hours, or overnight. Drain and rinse again. Set aside.

Heat a large pot or Dutch oven over medium-high heat, then add the olive oil. Once the oil is hot, add the onion, carrots, and celery, and cook, stirring constantly, until the vegetables are golden brown. Add the garlic.

Season the boar with salt and pepper, brown in a separate pan, then add it to the pot. Pour in the stock, adding more if needed to cover. Bring to a boil, reduce the heat to low, cover, and simmer slowly for about 2 hours. The stew should simmer (not boil) at all times.

After 2 hours, add the beans and pumpkin. Stir well and re-cover. Once the stew comes to a good simmer, remove the lid and cook for another 45 minutes. Stir frequently, and add more stock as needed to keep the stew from getting too dry. The stew will be done after about 3 hours total.

▶ **SERVING TIP** Just before serving, fold in the radicchio. Ladle into bowls and top with salsa verde. —C.K.

ESSENTIAL KITCHEN TOOLS

An underappreciated joy of cooking is the chance to work with tools. As with fishing tackle and hunting gear, there are now more kitchen tools out there than you could imagine—or possibly need. But with just these bare essentials, there's not a recipe in this book you can't make. One last thing: You'll notice this list is missing the most essential of kitchen tools—the knife. This was by design. We've reserved a special place for it on page 146.

POULTRY SHEARS

WHISK

MEASURING SET (CUPS AND SPOONS)

SPATULA

DUTCH OVEN

MEAT THERMOMETER

CAST IRON SKILLET

WOODEN SPOON

STOCKPOT

GRATER

METAL TONGS

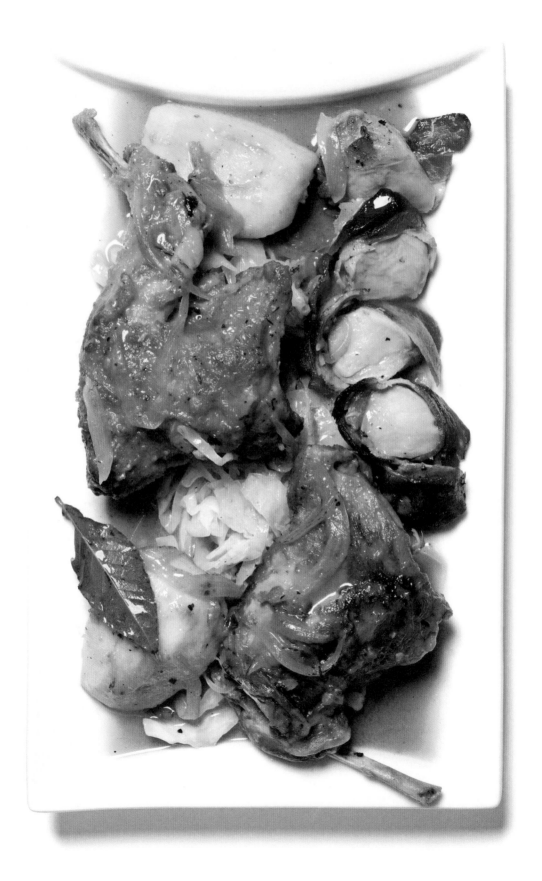

CIDER-BRAISED RABBIT WITH APPLES & CRÈME FRAÎCHE

Early fall yields two bumper crops—crisp apples and cottontails. Here's a recipe that puts both to use, in old French style, with the rabbits getting a long, slow braise in hard cider. Though it adds an extra step, cooking the loin separately ensures that each part of the rabbit is cooked to perfection. Sautéed cabbage makes an excellent accompaniment.

SERVES 4–6

Flour for dredging

2 rabbits, cut into serving pieces, loins reserved

Salt and freshly ground black pepper

5 tablespoons (3 fl oz/80 ml) vegetable oil

2 tablespoons unsalted butter

2 yellow onions, halved and thinly sliced crosswise

Bouquet garni of 4 Italian parsley sprigs, 4 thyme sprigs, and a bay leaf, tied together with kitchen twine

2 tablespoons Calvados or applejack

4 cups (32 fl oz/1 l) dry hard cider

2 cups (16 fl oz/500 ml) chicken stock

4 slices bacon or pancetta

2 Granny Smith apples, peeled, cored, and quartered

½ cup (4 fl oz/125 ml) crème fraîche or heavy cream

In a shallow bowl, season enough flour to dredge the rabbit with salt and pepper. Coat all the rabbit pieces except the loins in the flour mixture; shake off the excess and set aside.

In a large pot or Dutch oven over medium-high heat, heat 3 tablespoons of the vegetable oil. Add the dredged rabbit and brown it nicely, 2–3 minutes per side. Transfer to a plate.

Pour off the fat from the pot. Add the butter and onions; reduce the heat to medium-low. Sauté until the onions are well softened, about 12 minutes. Return the meat to the pot, along with the herbs and a generous sprinkling of salt and pepper. Cook for 2 minutes, then sprinkle the Calvados over the rabbit. Ignite the Calvados with a long-necked lighter (off the stove). When the flames subside, add the cider and stock. Bring to a boil, then reduce the heat to low, cover, and simmer gently until the rabbit is tender, about 1 hour and 15 minutes.

With a slotted spoon, remove the rabbit pieces to a platter and cover with foil. Discard the herbs. Cook the liquid over high heat until reduced by about half, about 20 minutes, occasionally skimming the surface.

As the sauce is reducing, wrap the reserved rabbit loins in the bacon, securing with toothpicks. Heat a skillet over high heat and add the remaining 2 tablespoons vegetable oil. Add the loins and cook until brown, about 4 minutes per side. Transfer to a cutting board and let rest for a few minutes before slicing thinly.

When the braising liquid is reduced, add the apples and cook until just tender. Gently add the crème fraîche or cream and stir to incorporate. Arrange the braised rabbit pieces and sliced loin on a platter with the apples, and top with the sauce.

▶ **DRINK PAIRING** With all the attention for artisanal microbrew beers, don't overlook another revolution in fermented beverages—hard cider. Big labels tend toward the sweet side, but for a richer, earthier flavor, try smaller brands such as Original Sin Hard Cider.

SALT-CRUSTED FISH

Nearly any fish can benefit from this impressive treatment. Double the recipe as needed, depending on the size of the fish and the appetites at the table, and feel free to adjust the herbs as desired. For an easy side, toss some cut potatoes in olive oil with salt and pepper, spread them in a roasting pan, and put the pan in with the fish.

SERVES 2–4

1 whole fish, gutted and scaled

Salt and freshly ground black pepper

2 sprigs tarragon

6 egg whites

3 cups (1½ lb/750 g) kosher salt

2 bay leaves, crumbled

Extra-virgin olive oil, for drizzling

1 lemon, cut into wedges

Preheat the oven to 450°F (230°C). Rinse the fish inside and out, and pat to dry. Sprinkle salt and pepper into the fish's cavity, then tuck the tarragon sprigs inside.

Whip the egg whites until stiff peaks form, then fold the 3 cups kosher salt and the bay leaves into the egg whites to form a thick paste.

Line a sheet pan with parchment paper. Spread about a third of the salt paste in the center of the parchment paper and lay the fish on the paste. With a rubber spatula, smear the remaining paste all over the fish so that it's completely encased. Place the pan in the oven.

Cook for about 25 minutes. By this time, the salt paste will have hardened into a thick crust. Allow the fish to rest 5–10 minutes, then crack the crust by knocking it with the flat side of a butter knife, and remove the crust in chunks.

▶ **SERVING TIP** Scoop out the meat, drizzling it with olive oil and giving it a squeeze or two of lemon.

BUTCHERING DEER

If field dressing is the last thing you do before the butcher hands you a box of white packages, you're missing out. If you see the hunting process all the way through, from lacing your boots to enjoying a forkful of venison, you'll truly learn where your meat comes from. And it'll be the best venison you've ever had.

SKINNING MADE SIMPLE

1 Use a knife with a thin, slightly flexible blade of 5–7 inches (13–18 cm). Lower the carcass on the gambrel so the hams are roughly eye level and the head is touching the ground, which helps keep the critter from swinging as you work.

2 At the groin, slip your knife's point under the skin, blade up, and cut a long slit from the bottom of one ham past the knee. Repeat on the other side.

3 Loosen the skin at each knee and cut around the joint. Peel the skin off the back legs to the tail, and use sharp lopping shears to cut the front legs off at the knee. Sever the tailbone and peel down to the shoulders, using your knife as necessary.

4 At the chest opening, slip your knife under the skin and cut a long slit along the inside of each front leg to the severed end. Peel the skin off the legs, then shoulders, then to the base of the neck, using your knife to help free the skin.

5 Slice through the meat of the neck with a knife, and cut through the spine with a saw.

BONING THE GOOD FROM THE BEST

1 Remove the head and wipe and rinse off any hair, mold, or blood with a vinegar-soaked cloth and cool water. Get two large, clean pans or buckets. One is for meat we'll categorize as Good—the fattier, more sinewy portions that will become burger, sausage, jerky, stew meat, and pot roast (see "The Cut Chart," below). And the second for Best—the larger, leaner, more tender cuts that make steaks, roasts, and kabobs.

2 Detach the front legs: Grab a shank, pull it slightly away from the body, and start slicing between the leg and the rib cage. Continue cutting around the leg, eventually between the shoulder blade and the back. A sharp knife will make this surprisingly easy. Repeat on the other side, and set aside.

3 Remove neck meat, brisket, and flank and toss into the Good pan. Next, remove the backstraps. For each, cut two long slits from the rump to the base of the neck—one along the backbone, the other along the top of the ribs. Make a horizontal cut across these two slits at the base of the neck, and lift the backstrap while scraping along the bone beneath with your knife to collect as much meat as possible. Toss into the Best pan.

4 Take off the shank meat on each hind leg and add to the Good pan. On the rest of the hindquarter, seams of silverskin run between large muscles. It's easiest to first separate these muscles as much as possible by working wet fingers into the seams. Then cut the muscles off the bone to get clean, near-seamless hunks of meat, all of which goes in the Best pan.

5 Cut the shank meat from the front legs and toss into the Good pan. The upper portion of each front shoulder does have some reasonably sinew-free meat that can be used for roasts or even steaks—just not very good ones. Put this, as well as any remaining edible meat on the carcass, into the Good pan.

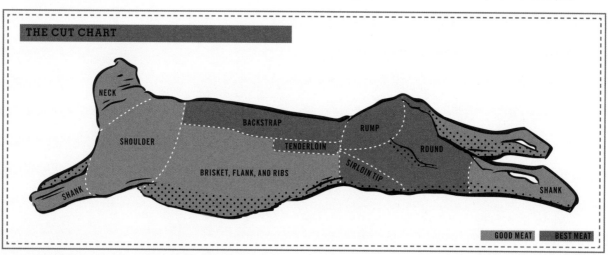

THE CUT CHART

NECK

BACKSTRAP

SHOULDER

RUMP

TENDERLOIN

ROUND

BRISKET, FLANK, AND RIBS

SIRLOIN TIP

SHANK

SHANK

GOOD MEAT   BEST MEAT

TRIMMED TO PERFECTION

1 Assess each piece of meat in the Good pan. It's okay to have small amounts of silverskin and fat in burger or sausage, but you want very little in jerky and stew meat. If the piece can be trimmed into a clean hunk of lean meat, trim and start a pile designated for jerky/stew. If not, trim the fat as best you can (leave the silverskin) and toss into a second pile.

2 Now trim every last bit of fat from each Best cut. If you expect your venison to be in the freezer for longer than 6 months, leave the silverskin for now and trim it later, as it can help protect the meat from freezer burn. Otherwise, cut it off.

3 Instead of cutting steaks at this point, thereby limiting your future options, cut the backstraps into sections 10–12 inches (25–30 cm) long, leave the individual muscles of the hindquarter whole, and freeze it all like that. When you take a package out to thaw and cook, you'll still have the option of making medallions, steaks, fillets, or whole dry roasts. —D.H.

OPEN A BASEMENT BUTCHER SHOP

Butchering a deer can be a chore that will make a mess of the area—in this case, your basement—and send you limping back up the steps with a backache. But there's a better way to take care of that animal—and yourself.

This DIY butchering table will make your trimming and grinding (and meat cutting in general) a more pleasant experience. It has the added benefits of being dirt cheap to source and build, easy to store and clean, and large enough for two people to work at together. Plus, to avoid the back pain, it can be raised to a spine-pleasing height. Before butchering, clean the table with a 50/50 mix of bleach and water. Rinse with distilled water. You'll be cranking out perfect cuts and beautifully ground wild meat in no time. —T.E.N.

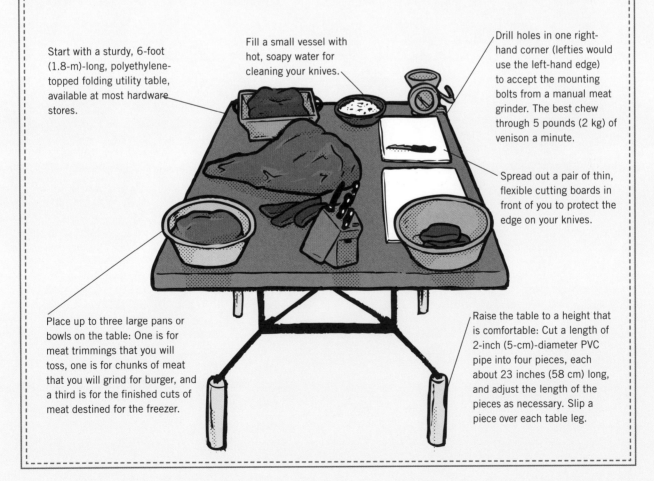

Start with a sturdy, 6-foot (1.8-m)-long, polyethylene-topped folding utility table, available at most hardware stores.

Fill a small vessel with hot, soapy water for cleaning your knives.

Drill holes in one right-hand corner (lefties would use the left-hand edge) to accept the mounting bolts from a manual meat grinder. The best chew through 5 pounds (2 kg) of venison a minute.

Spread out a pair of thin, flexible cutting boards in front of you to protect the edge on your knives.

Place up to three large pans or bowls on the table: One is for meat trimmings that you will toss, one is for chunks of meat that you will grind for burger, and a third is for the finished cuts of meat destined for the freezer.

Raise the table to a height that is comfortable: Cut a length of 2-inch (5-cm)-diameter PVC pipe into four pieces, each about 23 inches (58 cm) long, and adjust the length of the pieces as necessary. Slip a piece over each table leg.

VENISON-STUFFED TAMALES

Chef John Currence of City Grocery in Oxford, Mississippi, finds that the rich taste of venison makes a great complement to traditional tamale flavors. All told, you'll need several hours to make this dish. What won't take long is cleaning your plate.

STUFFING

2 cups (⅓ lb/5 oz/155 g) chopped bacon

Salt and freshly ground black pepper

3 lb (1.5 kg) venison shoulder, cubed

1 cup (5 oz/155 g) flour, seasoned with onion powder and paprika

1 large yellow onion, diced

2 ribs celery, diced

2 carrots, peeled and diced

2 jalapeño chiles, or more to taste

8 garlic cloves, crushed

4 tomatoes, cored, seeded, and chopped

2 teaspoons red pepper flakes

½ teaspoon cinnamon

1 tablespoon cocoa powder

1½ tablespoons cumin seeds, toasted and crushed

½ cup (4 fl oz/125 ml) tequila

3 tablespoons lime juice

4 cups (32 fl oz/1 l) chicken broth

⅓ cup (½ oz/15 g) chopped cilantro

Tabasco sauce

DOUGH

¼ cup (2 oz/60 g) lard

4 tablespoons (2 oz/60 g) butter

1 teaspoon baking powder

2 cups (11 oz/345 g) masa harina

¾ cup (6 fl oz/180 ml) heated chicken stock

½ red onion, finely diced

½ tablespoon puréed garlic

2 cups (12 oz/375 g) roasted corn kernels

½ tablespoon ground cumin, toasted

15–20 dried cornhusks

MAKE THE STUFFING In a Dutch oven over medium heat, cook the bacon. Remove from the pot with a slotted spoon, reserving the drippings.

Salt and pepper the venison, then dust lightly with the seasoned flour, shaking off the excess. Over medium-low heat, brown the meat in the bacon fat in small batches. Remove and reserve. Add vegetable oil as needed to cook the onion, celery, carrots, jalapeños, and garlic. Stir them into the pot and sauté until softened, about 10 minutes.

Add the tomatoes and season with salt and pepper. Return the bacon and venison to the pot, and stir in the red pepper flakes, cinnamon, cocoa powder, and cumin. Add the tequila and lime juice, and bring to a simmer while stirring. Add the broth and return to a simmer. Cover the Dutch oven and simmer over low heat for about 3½ hours, checking periodically and adding water if needed to make sure it doesn't dry out. When the venison is tender, remove it from the heat and let cool. Pour off any excess liquid, reserving it for later, and pull the venison apart with two forks. Stir in the cilantro and season with salt, pepper, and Tabasco to taste.

MAKE THE DOUGH In a mixer, beat the lard and butter with the baking powder until light in texture. Slowly add the masa harina until fully incorporated. Beat in the hot stock. The dough should reach the consistency of thick cake batter. Stir in the onion, garlic, corn, and cumin. Season to taste with salt and pepper.

ASSEMBLE THE TAMALES Soak the cornhusks in warm water for 10 minutes. Lay one whole husk flat on a cutting board. In the center of the husk, place about 3½–4 tablespoons tamale dough. Press it out into a rectangle about ⅜ inch (1 cm) thick. (This should leave you about 1 inch/2½ cm from the edges.) Spoon about 2 tablespoons venison filling along the center of the dough. Grab the husk on a long side and gently roll it over the top. The dough should close over and seal in the filling. Roll the tamale tightly, then grab the husk ends and twist gently, like wrapping a piece of candy. Tear a cornhusk along the grain to make threads to tie the tamale ends. Repeat until all dough is used. Put the tamales in a steamer basket set in a pot with water beneath it and steam, covered, for 35 minutes. Serve at once. —C.K.

THE JOY OF SQUIRRELS

When the overhauled edition of the *Joy of Cooking* was published in 1997, the venerable bible of American home cooks featured more than a thousand new recipes said to reflect the country's changing tastes. Quietly omitted, however, were the illustrated instructions for skinning and cooking squirrels, which had been a mainstay of the book for close to six decades. The message, alas, was clear: America had gone from being the land of burgoo to being the land of burritos, and a meat relished by culinary icons such as James Beard and Julia Child ("delicious," she decreed) had slipped off the nation's kitchen radar.

It would be easy to draw a distinction between the kitchens of hunters and those of nonhunters (which presumably includes the *Joy of Cooking*'s test kitchen), and thus dismiss the omission as merely one more slight against hunters—except that sportsmen aren't eating as many squirrels, either. Not long ago, an 11-year study by the Illinois Natural History Survey discovered a more than 30 percent decrease in the number of resident squirrel hunters—figures backed up by federal statistics, which have shown a steady decline since the 1970s. This is good news if you happen to be a squirrel, but disheartening if, like me, you consider squirrel to be one of the wild's tastiest menu items. It's a dark, sweet, nut-infused meat that falls somewhere between grouse and rabbit but—if I may go out on a limb here—bests both.

Why aren't we eating more squirrels? Two reasons: First, more hunters are setting their sights exclusively on big game, tramping through squirrel-choked woods in search of whitetails. Second, improperly prepared squirrel—mishandled in the cleaning or cooking or both—often spells disaster on the plate. And if hunters aren't motivated by the promise of a first-rate meal ahead . . . well, they might just sleep in until deer season.

That second reason is easily remedied. Squirrel cookery begins in the field: The moment you retrieve your downed squirrel, your cooking method will be apparent. Old squirrels, which have notoriously tough meat, require braising or stewing to break down the stringy flesh. Young ones, small enough to tuck into a pocket, are tender and more appropriate for frying or roasting. If the squirrel's age isn't evident by its size, I abide by the white-hair rule: White in the muzzle fur or on the rear legs means it's older and destined for the stewpot. You can also check the teeth and claws; if they're worn down, stew it.

Once the squirrel has been skinned, cleaned, and butchered (and any shotgun pellets dug out), soak it overnight in a brine. Salted water will suffice, but you'll get better results by combining ½ cup each of salt, pepper, and brown sugar with 1 gallon of water. Now you're ready to cook.

HOW TO STEW SQUIRREL CHOWDER

Brunswick stew, the classic squirrel dish, was allegedly invented in either Brunswick County, Virginia, or Brunswick, Georgia. The dispute, like the stew, is long simmering. The humorist Roy Blount, Jr. claims it wasn't *invented* at all: "Brunswick stew is what happens when small mammals carrying ears of corn fall into barbecue pits."

Whatever its provenance, it's a hearty medley of squirrel, corn, lima beans, tomatoes, and whatever else you're inclined to toss in the cauldron.

Or you can dish up your squirrels the way Mac English, the 77-year-old hunter behind the squirrel-dog revival in South Carolina's Piedmont Woods, does. His New England–style cream-based chowder draws crowds at his regular squirrel feasts. "Squirrel chowder is the way to eat a squirrel," says English.

Bring 10 cups (80 fl oz/2½ l) squirrel stock or beef stock to a boil in a large pot. Dice 5 medium potatoes, 2 yellow onions, 2 ribs celery, and 2 carrots, and add them to the pot, along with 1 teaspoon each salt and pepper, 1 teaspoon garlic powder, and 2 cubes chicken bouillon. Reduce the heat and simmer until the vegetables are tender. Add the meat of 4 to 8 squirrels that you have previously pressure-cooked or parboiled and then boned, and simmer for 10 minutes. Add 4 tablespoons (2 oz/60 g) butter, 8 oz (250 g) Velveeta cheese, and 4 oz (125 g) cream cheese, and simmer, stirring, until the cheese melts. Stir in 1 pint (16 fl oz/500 ml) half-and-half and 2 cans (5 oz/155-g) evaporated milk, and warm through. —T.E.N.

LARRY BROWN'S SQUIRREL, BISCUITS & GRAVY

The late Larry Brown, hunter and author of several works of classic Southern literature, had a saying when things were difficult, complicated, aggravating, or vexing in some way: "They ain't squirrels, baby." Because squirrels, for Larry, were the antithesis of all that: They were a joy to hunt, a joy to cook, a joy to eat, and hunting and eating them was one of the simple pleasures that gave meaning to his life. On numerous mornings he greeted me with a plate of squirrel, biscuits, and gravy, his signature dish, usually made with squirrels his sons had killed, since Larry's workload, late in life, tended to keep him out of the woods. Nothing ever tasted better.

SERVES 4

2 squirrels (about 1 lb/500 g each), dressed and quartered

5 slices bacon

⅔ cup (4 oz/125 g) all-purpose flour for dredging, plus ¼ cup (1½ oz/45 g) for gravy

Salt and freshly ground black pepper

BISCUITS

2 cups (10 oz/315 g) all-purpose flour

1 teaspoon sugar

1 teaspoon salt

2 teaspoons baking powder

½ teaspoon baking soda

½ cup (95 g/3 oz) chilled vegetable shortening

¾ cup (6 fl oz/180 ml) buttermilk

3 tablespoons (2 oz/60 g) melted butter

Parboil the squirrel pieces: Place them in a large pot and add enough salted water to cover. Bring to a simmer and cook until the meat is very tender but still intact, 1–2 hours. Remove the squirrel pieces from the water and set aside to cool.

In a large cast iron skillet or Dutch oven, fry the bacon slices over medium heat until the bacon is crispy and all the fat has been rendered. Reserve for another use. In a wide, shallow bowl or pan, season ⅔ cup of the flour (or more as needed) with salt and pepper. Dredge the squirrel pieces in the flour, shaking off any excess, and add to the bacon grease. Reduce heat to medium-low and cook the squirrel until lightly browned, about 10 minutes per side. Work in batches and add butter to the pan if needed.

Meanwhile, make the biscuits. Preheat the oven to 400°F (200°C). Mix the dry ingredients in a bowl. Divide the shortening into several pieces and cut into the dry ingredients until the mixture resembles coarse crumbs. Make a hole in the center and pour in the buttermilk. Using your hands, fold the dry mixture into the buttermilk until you have a sticky dough. Turn the dough onto a floured surface and fold it over on itself to form layers. Flatten it with your hands until it's about ¾-inch thick. Using a biscuit cutter or glass, cut out rounds. Transfer to a sheet pan and brush with the melted butter. Bake for 15 minutes until golden brown.

When the squirrel pieces are finished, remove to a plate or keep warm in a low-heat oven. Pour off the excess grease in the pan, keeping about ¼ cup. Increase the heat to medium-high and add ¼ cup flour, stirring constantly and scraping up any browned bits, until the mixture turns an oaky shade of brown. Add ¾ cup cold water and stir until a thick gravy forms; if it's too thick, add additional water. Salt and pepper to taste. Serve the squirrel and biscuits with the gravy on the side.

GRILL-ROASTED FISH ON THE HALF SHELL

Donald Link, chef and owner of the stellar Herbsaint and Cochon restaurants in New Orleans, once conducted an experiment with some largemouths he'd caught. One fillet he cooked without the skin; another, skin on but scaled; and another, skin on and unscaled. "The difference in moisture was like night and day," he says of the last fillet. This technique for grill-roasting fish is called "fisherman's style" or "fish on the half shell." Says Donald, "The beauty of it is the simplicity. You can cook it outdoors, and you don't even have to gut the fish. Just take off the side."

SERVES 6

Six 7-oz (220-g) fish fillets (bass, redfish, or pretty much any fish), skin and scales on, pinbones removed

Kosher salt and freshly ground black pepper

Red pepper flakes

½ cup (4 fl oz/125 ml) extra-virgin olive oil

½ cup (¾ oz/20 g) chopped Italian parsley

2 large lemons

Rinse the fish fillets and pat dry. Place them on a baking sheet and season each fillet with ¼ teaspoon each salt, pepper, and red pepper flakes. Drizzle half of the olive oil over the fillets. Use your fingers to distribute the oil and seasonings evenly, then set aside to marinate while you heat up the grill.

Start a medium-hot fire (375°F/190°C) in your grill. When the grill is ready, place the fillets, scale-side down, on the hot grate. Don't move them or the skin will stick. Cover the grill until the fish is just cooked through, 7–10 minutes. (It will easily flake when tested with a paring knife.)

Using a metal spatula, transfer the cooked fillets to serving plates and sprinkle generously with salt, parsley, and remaining olive oil. Cut the lemons in half and squeeze the juice (through a small strainer or your fist to catch the seeds) evenly over the fish. Serve immediately.

PARTRIDGE TWO WAYS

Sean Brock, a James Beard Award–winning chef from Charleston, South Carolina, likes to cook the legs and breasts of gamebirds separately—the legs poached in fat, the breasts seared—to produce tender dark meat and moist, crispy-skinned white meat.

SERVES 4

4 chukar partridges or other upland birds

At least 2 cups (16 fl oz/500 ml) olive oil

ALMOND CREAM*

¾ cup (3½ oz/105 g) slivered almonds

1½ cups (12 fl oz/375 ml) cream

HUCKLEBERRY SAUCE*

2 tablespoons olive oil

1 carrot, chopped

1 rib celery, chopped

½ yellow onion, chopped

½ cup (4 fl oz/125 ml) port wine

2 cups (16 fl oz/500 ml) chicken stock

1 cup (4 oz/125 g) huckleberries or blackberries

2 tablespoons butter

Salt and freshly ground black pepper

2 tablespoons olive oil

*Almond cream must be made several hours ahead, or it may be made 1 day ahead, along with the huckleberry sauce.

Preheat the oven to 275°F (135°C). With a sharp knife, remove the legs with the thighs attached from the partridges. Remove and discard the wings. Breast the birds (see page 96), and refrigerate that meat until later. Place the legs in a loaf pan or other pan that will hold them snugly. Cover with olive oil, using as much as needed to submerge the legs. Cook in the oven until the meat is tender enough to fall off the bones, 1½–2 hours. Remove the legs from the oil, let cool, and refrigerate until ready to use.

MAKE THE ALMOND CREAM Spread the almonds in a heavy skillet over medium heat and shake or stir them until just golden. Reserve one-third of the almonds, and place the rest in a saucepan with the cream. Bring to a simmer over medium heat, stirring, then remove. Let the mixture steep for several hours in the refrigerator. With the reserved almonds, make a powder by pulsing them in a spice mill or food processor.

MAKE THE HUCKLEBERRY SAUCE Heat 2 tablespoons olive oil in a saucepan over medium-high heat. Sauté the carrot, celery, and onion until very tender, 8–10 minutes. Add the port and cook, stirring, until the liquid is nearly evaporated. Add the stock and half of the berries and bring to a boil. Reduce the heat and simmer until the liquid is reduced by half. Strain the sauce, discarding the vegetables, and return to the stove. Whisk in the butter, season with salt and pepper to taste, and keep warm.

About 30 minutes before serving, preheat the oven to 350°F (180°C). Strain the almond cream, discarding the almonds, and gently warm in a saucepan. Put the reserved chukar legs in a pan and reheat them in the oven. Add the remaining berries to the sauce and return it to a simmer.

Now on to the partridge breasts. Heat 2 tablespoons olive oil in a sauté pan over medium-high heat. Season the breasts with salt and pepper and set them, skin side down, to sear until the skin is brown and crispy. Then flip the breasts and continue to cook for several more minutes, until the meat is cooked through. (Slice into one to check. The meat should have a faint blush of pinkness remaining.)

▶ **SERVING TIP** Pour about ⅓ cup (3 fl oz/80 ml) of the warmed almond cream onto each plate. Top with the partridge legs and breast. Spoon the sauce over the partridge, berries and all, and finish with a dusting of the reserved almond powder. Serve at once.

IRISH ANGLER'S PIE

I caught the largest lake trout of my life on a cold and drizzly early-spring day in County Galway, Ireland, one day before my wedding. My future father-in-law was fishing with me, not enjoying the cold one bit, and when I finally landed my trout (it was the only fish we caught that day), I told him I was ready to call it a day. "My feet are getting cold," I said, meaning it literally. "Son," came his reply, "that's one phrase you don't need to be using today." We took the trout back to the inn where we were staying, where it was smoked and served the next morning for breakfast, but this traditional Irish dish—a variation of the pub classic shepherd's pie, using fish rather than lamb or beef—would have been even better: a thick, piping-hot stew of ale-poached trout, leeks, and mushrooms topped with an oven-browned crust of chive mashed potatoes and Irish cheddar. It's the ideal remedy for cold feet—of any kind.

SERVES 4

TOPPING

1 ½ lbs (750 g) potatoes, peeled and cut into 1-inch pieces

¾ cup (6 gl oz/180 ml) milk

3 tablespoons butter

2 tablespoons chopped fresh chives

Salt and freshly ground black pepper

1 lb (500 g) lake trout fillets (or fillets from any mild, flaky fish)

2 bay leaves

1 cup (8 fl oz/250 ml) milk

1 cup (8 fl oz/250 ml) Guinness ale

4 tablespoons (2 oz/60 g) butter

3 large leeks, washed and roughly chopped

1 cup (3 oz/90 g) chopped shiitake mushrooms, stems removed

2 tablespoons flour

1½ teaspoons Coleman's mustard

2 tablespoons freshly squeezed lemon juice

2 hard-boiled eggs, chopped

¾ cup (3 oz/90 g) freshly grated Irish or white Cheddar cheese

Dash of paprika

MAKE THE TOPPING In a medium saucepan, cover the potatoes with salted water and bring to a boil. Reduce the heat to a simmer and cook about 15 minutes, or until you can easily pierce the potatoes with a fork. Drain in a colander, then return to the pan and cook for another minute, to steam off any excess moisture. Add the milk and butter and mash until creamy and smooth. Add the chives and salt and pepper to taste, and stir until well blended. Set aside.

MAKE THE FISH Preheat the oven to 400°F (200°C). Place the trout fillets and bay leaves in a shallow pan and cover with the milk and the Guinness. Put the pan in the oven and cook for about 15 minutes, or until the trout begins to flake.

While the trout is cooking, melt the butter in a large sauté pan over medium heat. Add the leeks and cook until just tender, about 8 minutes. Add the mushrooms and continue cooking, another 4 minutes. Stir in the flour and continue stirring for another minute, then remove from the heat.

ASSEMBLE THE PIE When the fish is done, remove the fillets with a slotted spoon and set aside. Discard the bay leaves. Return the leek mixture to the stove over medium-low heat, and add the cooking liquid. Stir frequently until the mixture thickens, about 10 minutes, then add the mustard, lemon juice, eggs, and salt and pepper to taste. Flake the fish and add to the mixture.

Spoon the mixture into an ovenproof dish. Top with the reserved mashed potatoes, using a fork to create an uneven, craggy surface (the more bumps, the more browning you'll get). Sprinkle the grated cheese over the potatoes and dust with paprika. Cook in the oven for about 30 minutes, or until the mixture is bubbly and the topping is browned and crusty.

VENISON PIEROGI

Bob Matuszewski, a third-generation butcher and sausagemaker who owns the Quaker Creek Store in Pine Island, New York, makes his venison pierogi (Polish pasta pockets akin to ravioli) the same way his grandmother did, by stuffing a simple dough with a mixture of venison, chopped onion, and butter, then frying it in butter and serving it alongside some onions sautéed in the same butter. Take a bite, and you're instantly transported to the hearty end of a red stag hunt in the mountains of Poland—pretty good mileage for a few ounces of ground venison.

SERVES 4

FILLING
1 onion, finely chopped
1 tablespoon butter
Salt and freshly ground black pepper
¼ lb (125 g) ground venison, browned

DOUGH
2 cups (10 oz/315 g) flour
2 large eggs
½ cup (4 fl oz/125 ml) water
½ teaspoon salt

MAKE THE FILLING In a medium sauté pan or skillet, sauté the onion in the butter until translucent, and then season to taste with salt and pepper. Mix with the venison, and set aside to let cool.

MAKE THE DOUGH Mound the flour on a kneading board (or any nonstick counter surface, like marble or Corian) and mold a hole in the center. Drop the eggs into the hole and cut the eggs into the flour with a knife. Add the water and salt and knead the dough until firm. Cover with a warm towel (you can microwave a towel for 10 seconds or so), and let rest 10 minutes. Divide the dough into two halves and roll out the halves until thin. With a biscuit cutter or wide glass, cut the dough into rounds.

ASSEMBLE THE PIEROGI Spoon a dollop of filling onto the middle of each round. Moisten the edges of the rounds with water, fold the dough over so the rounds are folded in half, and firmly seal the edges together with the tines of a fork. (Be sure they're very well sealed, so that they don't open up while cooking.)

Drop the pierogi into boiling salted water and cook about 4 minutes. Remove from the water with a slotted spoon.

When ready to serve, heat a few pats of butter over medium heat. Sauté the pierogi on both sides until golden brown. If desired, serve with onions sautéed in a few more pats of butter.

ADVENTURES IN VENISON

At the deer camp I used to frequent near Crystal Springs, Mississippi, we called it "the autopsy": In an open-sided shed, the deer would be hoisted up by its hind legs on a gambrel and inspected by our camp butcher and amateur forensic expert, Bill Peavey. An irascible man, tough as a camp skillet, Peavey always took meticulous care in showing us precisely where and how our bullets had penetrated the deer and, more important, where we should have aimed those bullets to avoid damaging the meat. Lesson completed, he'd begin butchering the deer by slicing out the entrails, along with the heart, liver, kidneys, and other organs, letting them all drop into a 25-gallon plastic "gutbucket" that he'd later haul off on his four-wheeler to a distant fenceline—a gift to the local coyotes. Once, watching a gorgeous purple liver hit the bucket with a forlorn splat, I voiced a meek protest, but Peavey would hear none of it. I might as well have asked if I could steam an antler for breakfast. To him, the organs weren't meat: They were scraps. Away went the gutbucket, and with it the gorgeous liver.

The Swahili have a saying: "Every meat is meat." The backstraps, roasts, steaks, and other assorted muscle cuts may be delicious—and for me and many others, a primary reason for hunting—but they're only a start. Inside that humble gutbucket, amid the inedibles, is a wild set of eating pleasures. For some folks, this is hardly news—eating the heart remains a post-kill tradition in some deer camps, and there are those who still celebrate a successful hunt with a plate of venison liver and onions. These hunters were once scarce, but today an appreciation for organs has risen from the ashes.

Offal—an all-encompassing title for the edible organs of an animal, otherwise known as "variety meats" or, more nobly, viscera—has disappeared from household supper tables in the last century, and so too has it faded from the dinged-up dinner-and-poker tables of this nation's deer camps. Perhaps the American culture's squeamishness spilled over into the hunting world, maybe laziness was to blame, or it could just be the benign neglect that comes from living in a prepackaged, vacuum-packed age.

But as restaurant-goers are slowly rediscovering the joys of eating offal—cheeks, tripe, brains, and marrow have become staples at chic urban restaurants—so too are hunters, who have access to the freshest organs and, in the case of venison and other game, to some of the rarest and most prized cuts of meat. No longer is the gutbucket the end of the line. Now is the time to branch out—and eat up.

THE PLEASURES OF EATING OFFAL

"It seems only polite to the animal you've killed," says Fergus Henderson, the legendary London chef widely credited with rescuing offal from the culinary gutbucket and the author of *The Whole Beast: Nose to Tail Eating*, a cult-classic cookbook on both sides of the pond. "And it's all fantastic," he continues, "the brains and tongue and liver and kidneys and all the other bits. There's a texture and unctuous flavor to them that nothing else can quite match. And it just makes so much sense to eat them, especially if you're a hunter. At my restaurant, people can't get enough of venison offal. They munch it up happily."

What Henderson calls nose-to-tail eating is, like hunting, about encountering the wilderness in all its visceral glory. The heart, liver, kidneys, and tongue are prize cuts. Eating the heart is a meaningful celebration, while the liver is more well known in some circles, as it's famously easy to cook. All you need is a skillet and a pat of butter for a great camp dinner.

Kidneys can be a tough sell for many people—"liver squared" would be an apt description of their taste. (Anecdotal evidence: Lamb kidneys were served at my wedding dinner, and I think I was the only one who ate them.)

Last but not least, there's the tongue. Here I think it's all in the looks—what you see on the plate isn't that far off from what you see in the mirror. But we should get over our squeamishness: Venison tongue, like that of any ungulate, is a lean, boneless muscle that's packed with protein, a sublime texture, and great meaty flavor.

GRILLED MARINATED VENISON HEART

"The heart," says British chef Fergus Henderson, "encapsulates the beast that it comes from—
the whole essence of the animal is in there." Hence the Native American tradition of eating the
warm heart of your prey in order to gain its spirit. For a muscle that never stops working, the heart
is surprisingly tender, "firm and meaty but giving," says Henderson, "with just the right amount of
bite." Besides containing your deer's spiritual essence, the heart is also loaded with protein and
B vitamins and contains very little fat. In this recipe, Henderson marinates the heart in a simple
mixture of balsamic vinegar, thyme, and salt and pepper, and then sears it quickly over a hot fire.
For a variation, amp up the marinade with some ground chile peppers and cumin seed in the style
of Peruvian *anticuchos*, the grilled skewers of beef heart that street vendors hawk in Lima.

SERVES 2–4 AS AN APPETIZER

1 venison heart

Chopped fresh thyme

Coarse sea salt and freshly ground
black pepper

A healthy splash of balsamic vinegar

Trim the heart of anything that looks like sinew (this is easy enough to
spot) and excess fat (which tends to be around the open top of the heart),
and remove any blood clots lurking in the ventricles. Slice the heart open
in order to lay it flat and complete the process. You want pieces 1 inch
(2.5 cm) square and up to ¼ inch (6 mm) thick; if the flesh is thicker than
that, slice horizontally through the meat before cutting the squares.

Toss the pieces of the heart with a generous sprinkling of salt, pepper, and
thyme. Drizzle with the vinegar. Refrigerate and let marinate for 24 hours.

Let the heart stand at room temperature for 30 minutes while you start
the grill. Cook the pieces on an oiled grill grate over a very hot fire for
about 1½ minutes per side. (They're best served somewhere between
medium-rare and medium. Overcooking produces tough squares
resembling jerky.) Serve warm, with a salad of watercress or white beans
and shallots.

▶ **BUTCHERING NOTES** The heart is easy to identify and easy to trim—just
cut away anything that doesn't look like muscle, slice it open, then trim
whatever light-colored, spongy-looking bits you might have missed. As
with all organ meats, try to cook the heart as soon as possible. In a pinch,
however, it can be frozen.

SEARED VENISON LIVER WITH BACON & CARAMELIZED ONIONS

Of all the viscera represented here, liver is the most familiar to us. Many people, myself included, were raised on weekday suppers of calves' liver and onions, and in my experience, venison liver is the least-neglected organ meat among hunters. When butchering, avoid any venison liver that doesn't look purple-pink and evenly beautiful; if it's spotted or mottled, it could be diseased, so trash it or use it for catfish bait. Deer don't have gallbladders, so you don't need to get all surgical about removing the liver—just cut it out and trim away the obvious odds and ends. Freshness is key. Try to cook the liver the same day the deer was killed, or at least by the next day.

SERVES 4

8 oz (250 g) slab bacon, cut into
½-inch (12-mm) squares

3 red onions, peeled and thinly sliced

Coarse salt and freshly ground black
pepper

All-purpose flour for dredging

1 venison liver (about 1½ lb/750 g),
cut into 8 generous slices

3 tablespoons butter, plus 1 tablespoon

2 cups (16 fl oz/500 ml) Yukon Jack

3 tablespoons chopped Italian parsley

Heat a large skillet over low heat. Add the bacon and slowly cook until the fat is rendered and the meat is starting to crisp, 12–14 minutes. With a slotted spoon, remove the bacon onto a layer of paper towels to drain. Add the onions to the pan and cook, stirring occasionally, until they're soft and lightly browned, 16–18 minutes. Remove them to a bowl, season with salt and pepper, and set aside. (Reheat the bacon and onions in a warm oven or microwave just prior to serving.)

In a shallow dish, season flour with salt and pepper and dredge the liver slices, shaking off any excess. Pour off any remaining fat from the pan and wipe out the pan with a paper towel. Heat the 3 tablespoons of butter over medium-high heat until it begins to foam, and add 4 pieces of liver. Cook for about 3 minutes per side, or until slightly past medium-rare (cut into them to be sure), then remove them to a plate, covering it with foil to keep the slices warm. Repeat with the remaining 4 slices, adding more butter to the pan if needed.

Reduce the heat to medium-low and add the Yukon Jack to the pan. Once it's warmed—15 seconds or so later—remove the pan from the heat and ignite it with a long-handled match or long-necked lighter. (The flames will go high, so be careful.) Shake the pan lightly until the flames subside. Return the pan to the heat and simmer the Yukon Jack until it reduces to a syrup-like consistency, scraping up any browned bits lingering on the bottom of the pan.

To serve, place two liver slices on each plate and top with generous heaps of the warmed onions and bacon. Spoon the Yukon Jack reduction over the liver and garnish it with parsley.

VENISON STEAK & KIDNEY EMPANADAS

The recipe that follows is a gentle introduction to eating kidneys, a south-of-the-border variation on the famed British pub standard of steak-and-kidney pie. This is a great way to use the kidneys of a single deer, since a little goes a very long way. The culinary quality of venison kidneys can vary widely, with occasionally unpleasant results—don't cook those of an old deer or a rutting buck, as they can be seriously pungent. Kidneys are encased in a creamy, waxy fat called suet, which is easily removed by cutting into it and then peeling it away. Split the kidney lengthwise, strip off the thin membrane covering the kidney, cut out the bean-size core at its center, and prepare.

SERVES 4

DOUGH
1 cup (5½ oz/170 g) masa harina

½ cup (3½ oz/105 g) yellow cornmeal

½ cup (2½ oz/75 g) all-purpose flour

½ teaspoon baking powder

Salt and freshly ground black pepper

¼ teaspoon ground cumin, plus 1 teaspoon

¼ teaspoon chili powder, plus 1 teaspoon

1 tablespoon lard or shortening

1 cup (8 fl oz/250 ml) warm water

FILLING
½ lb (250 g) venison top round or any tender cut, sliced into ½-inch (12-mm) cubes

2 venison kidneys (about ¼ lb/125 g total), diced small

½ teaspoon crushed red pepper

½ teaspoon paprika

1½ tablespoons olive oil

½ yellow onion, finely chopped

1 poblano chile, finely chopped

2 cloves garlic, minced

1 cup (8 fl oz/250 ml) venison or beef stock, plus ¼ cup (2 fl oz/60 ml)

1 tablespoon cornstarch

1 large egg beaten with 2 tablespoons water

MAKE THE DOUGH Combine the masa harina, cornmeal, all-purpose flour, baking powder, ½ teaspoon salt, ½ teaspoon pepper, and ¼ teaspoon each of cumin and chili powder in a bowl. Mix in the lard and then the water, adding a little at a time, working it with your hands until a dough forms. Mold this mixture into a ball, wrap it tightly in plastic wrap, and refrigerate for at least 30 minutes.

MAKE THE FILLING In a small bowl, combine the top round and kidneys with the remaining teaspoon each of cumin and chili powder, along with the crushed red pepper and paprika. Season with salt and pepper.

Heat the olive oil in a sauté pan over medium-high heat. Add the seasoned meats, stirring until the pieces are well browned. Add the onion and poblano, and cook for an additional 3 minutes, until just softened, then add the garlic and cook for another minute. Pour in 1 cup stock and bring it to a simmer. In a small bowl, whisk together the remaining ¼ cup stock and the cornstarch. Add this to the pan and stir to incorporate. Simmer briefly until the liquid thickens to a gravylike consistency. Remove it from the heat and set aside.

ASSEMBLE THE EMPANADAS Preheat the oven to 375°F (190°C) and line a sheet pan with parchment or wax paper. Fetch the dough from the refrigerator and cut it into 8 equal-size pieces. With a rolling pin, roll out each portion of dough between sheets of plastic wrap into 8-inch (20-cm) circles. (Allow yourself some time here; this is a bit of grunt work.) Beat together the egg and water until frothy, and, working one by one, brush the dough rounds with the egg wash and place ¼ cup of the meat filling in the middle of each. Fold the round over into a semicircle (use the plastic wrap to avoid touching and cracking the dough). Seal the edges; if desired, crimp them with a fork. Brush the tops with more egg wash.

Place the empanadas on the prepared sheet pan and bake them until golden, 35–40 minutes. Serve them hot.

BRAISED VENISON TONGUE OVER RICE NOODLES

A deer's tongue is fairly small; that is to say, about the same size as yours, apart from being longer. You can freeze and collect them as the season goes on or, for this preparation, mix in some thinly sliced venison sirloin to flesh out the meat quotient. When butchering, cutting up through the bottom of the jaw, in the soft middle part, is the easiest way to get at the tongue. Use a sharp knife to detach it. This recipe is a deer-camp variation of Vietnamese pho, the hot, fragrant noodle soups made with beef, chicken, giblets, or pig hearts. The Vietnamese consider pho the ultimate restorative, and it's easy to see why—after a cold day in the stand, a bowl of this will instantly thaw your frozen bones.

SERVES 4

4 venison tongues (about 1 lb/ 500 g total)

1 teaspoon vegetable oil

5 cloves garlic, lightly smashed, peeled, and thinly sliced

2 cinnamon sticks

2 whole cloves

2 whole star anise

1 teaspoon spicy chili paste

½ cup (4 fl oz/125 ml) soy sauce

2 tablespoons Vietnamese or Thai fish sauce (optional)

One 3-inch (7.5-cm) piece fresh ginger

2 yellow onions, peeled and halved

8 oz (250 g) medium rice stick noodles*

8 oz (250 g) spinach, trimmed, rinsed, and drained

Cilantro leaves, sweet basil leaves, and/or minced green onions for garnish

*Rice stick noodles are available at Asian markets. You can substitute angel hair pasta if needed.

Bring a large pot of water to boil. Add the tongues, reduce the heat to low, and simmer slowly, covered, for about 2 hours. Remove the tongues with tongs, let rest until just cool enough to touch, and peel off the skin. (It will come off easier when the tongues are warm. If the skin still adheres, trim it with a paring knife.) Cut into ¼-inch (6-mm) slices, and set aside.

Heat the oil in a large pot over medium-high heat. Add the garlic, cinnamon, cloves, star anise, and chili paste, and sauté until fragrant— only 15 seconds or so. Then add 9 cups (72 fl oz/2¼ l) water, the soy sauce, and the fish sauce (if using), and bring to a boil. Put in the tongue slices and reduce the heat until you have a slow but steady simmer.

Using tongs, char the ginger and onion halves directly over a gas flame, until evenly scorched. (For electric stoves, heat a heavy dry skillet over high heat and sear the ginger and onion on all sides until nearly blackened.) Add these to the pot.

Let simmer, covered, for about 2 hours, or until the tongue slices are very tender. Remove the cinnamon sticks, star anise, ginger, and onions, reserving the onions.

Cook the noodles according to package directions, rinse, and drain. Chop the onions roughly and return them to the pot, along with the spinach. Bring to a boil, and then remove from the heat.

▶ **SERVING TIP** Divide the warm noodles among serving bowls and ladle the meat, broth, and spinach on top. If desired, garnish with cilantro leaves, whole or torn sweet basil leaves, and minced green onions.

BUTTERMILK-FRIED QUAIL WITH AJAX GRAVY

This is classic Southern fare from Amy Lott Crockett, chef-owner of Ajax Diner, a funky meat-and-three joint in Oxford, Mississippi. Add a glass of sweet tea and you're good to go.

SERVES 4

BUTTER BEANS
4 tablespoons (2 oz/60 g) butter

1 slice bacon, chopped

6 cups (2½ lb/1.25 kg) fresh butter beans*

1 cup (8 fl oz/250 ml) chicken stock

QUAIL
Oil for frying

2 cups (16 fl oz/500 ml) buttermilk

1 egg

3 cups (15 oz/470 g) all-purpose flour

Kosher salt and freshly ground black pepper

12 whole quail, rinsed and patted dry

GRAVY
½ cup (2½ oz/75 g) all-purpose flour

3 cups (24 fl oz/750 ml) chicken stock

1 tablespoon chopped fresh Italian parsley (optional)

*Butter beans are what Southerners call lima beans. Don't they sound more delicious as butter beans?

MAKE THE BUTTER BEANS Melt the butter in a pot over medium heat. Add the chopped bacon and cook, stirring occasionally, until browned. Stir in the remaining ingredients, add water to cover, stir again, and bring to a boil. Reduce the heat to low, cover, and simmer the beans until tender, about 45 minutes. Set aside.

MAKE THE QUAIL In a large cast-iron skillet (or a deep fryer), heat several inches of oil to 350°F (180°C).

While the oil is heating, whisk the buttermilk with the egg until smooth. Spread the flour on a plate, and season with a tablespoon each of salt and pepper.

Dunk the quail in the buttermilk-egg wash, shaking off any excess, and then roll them in the flour mixture, coating evenly. Shake off any excess, and carefully place the quail in the hot oil. Fry until the thickest part of the breast reaches 165°F (74°C), about 7 minutes. Remove to paper towels to drain, then place in an oven set at a low temperature to keep warm until ready to serve.

MAKE THE GRAVY Discard all but ½ cup (4 fl oz/125 ml) of the cooking oil and return the skillet to the stove over medium heat. Add the flour and cook, stirring, until the mixture is medium brown and looks like milk chocolate. You can easily burn the flour; reduce the heat if it begins to smoke, and keep stirring. Gradually whisk in the chicken stock, and continue to whisk until the mixture has thickened into a gravy. Add the parsley, if using, and generous dashes of salt and pepper to taste.

▶ **SERVING TIP** Spoon the gravy on top of the quail, add a little salt and pepper, and pile a heap of butter beans on the side.

BLACKENED VENISON STEAKS

New Orleans's Commander's Palace, where Tory McPhail is the executive chef, is one of the country's most storied restaurants, thanks to putting a pair of devoted hunters and anglers in charge (Ti Adelaide Martin is a managing partner). For game and fish eaters, it's something like paradise. Here's one of their venison favorites.

SERVES 4

½ cup (4 fl oz/125 ml) dry red wine

½ cup (4 fl oz/125 ml) cane syrup

¼ teaspoon freshly ground black pepper

4 8-oz (250-g) venison steaks, about ½ inch (12 mm) thick

4 teaspoons Cajun spice blend

4 teaspoons vegetable oil

Bacon-Mashed Turnips (*far right*)

Combine the wine and cane syrup in a small saucepan over medium-high heat. Simmer gently until reduced by two-thirds, about 18 minutes. Remove from the heat and stir in the pepper.

Pat the venison steaks dry with kitchen towels (paper towels will stick). Sprinkle the Cajun seasoning on both sides.

Heat a large cast-iron skillet over medium-high heat until it is very hot and just smoking, 4–5 minutes. Add the oil, swirling to coat the bottom of the skillet. Once it's hot, sear the steaks until dark brown, 3–4 minutes. Turn the meat over, reduce the heat to medium, and sear 3–4 minutes for medium-rare.

Transfer the steaks to a platter and let rest 5–10 minutes. Serve them drizzled with the sauce, with the mashed turnips alongside.

WILD SIDE: BACON-MASHED TURNIPS

On their own, turnips can sometimes have a bitter flavor. However, when you smooth them out with plenty of milk and butter, and add some savory bacon (because bacon is always the answer), their true hearty character can shine through. Don't toss the leaves, either—turnip greens resemble mustard greens and are equally great. Smaller is better, but for larger leaves, you can replace the initial boiling water with fresh in order to ease the bitterness.

⅔ cup (4 oz/125 g) chopped bacon

1 cup (4 oz/125 g) chopped yellow onion

1 lb (500 g) small turnips, chopped

3 cups (24 fl oz/750 ml) milk

2 tablespoons unsalted butter, at room temperature

Salt and freshly ground black pepper

Heat a saucepan over medium heat. Cook the bacon, stirring, until the fat is rendered and the bacon is just beginning to color, about 4 minutes. Add the onion and cook, stirring occasionally, until soft, about another 4 minutes. Add the turnips and milk, bring to a simmer, and cook until tender, about 45 minutes. Drain in a colander. Return the mixture to the pan, add the butter, and season generously with salt and pepper. Stir vigorously with a heavy wooden spoon until roughly mashed.

SERVES 4

ROOT BEER–GLAZED DUCK BREAST

The rich flavors of duck meat have always attracted sweet, fruit-based sauces. Witness duck à l'orange, for instance. In this recipe, we forgo the fruit for something darker, woodsier, but no less sweet—root beer. Once it is reduced down to a saucy glaze, the root beer offers a tangy new twist on the classic combination. (Mashed sweet potatoes make a fine accompaniment.) It's incredibly easy but elegant enough to serve guests. And when they take their first bites, ask to see if they can guess the secret ingredient.

SERVES 4

Kosher salt

2 large whole duck breasts (mallard, pintail, canvasback), or 3 medium breasts (wood duck, wigeon)

4 teaspoons sesame seeds

½ cup (4 fl oz/125 ml) Barq's, Boylan, or other strong root beer

¼ cup (2 oz/60 g) brown sugar

2 tablespoons ketchup

1 teaspoon grated lemon zest

2 teaspoons Dijon mustard

Salt the duck breasts and let come to room temperature. (If using domestic, farm-raised ducks, score the skin with a sharp knife, in a crosshatch pattern.)

Meanwhile, toast the sesame seeds. Put the seeds in a small pan over medium heat. Shaking the pan occasionally, cook until the seeds turn golden and fragrant, about 3 minutes, being careful not to scorch them. Pour into a bowl and let cool.

Next, make the glaze. Combine the root beer, brown sugar, ketchup, lemon zest, and mustard in a small saucepan, and bring to a simmer over low heat. Cook, stirring often, until the mixture is saucy and coats the back of a spoon, about 10 minutes.

Heat a large sauté pan or grill pan over high heat until very hot. Pat the duck breasts dry with paper towels and lay them, skin side down, in the pan. Reduce the heat slightly, to medium-high, and cook undisturbed for about 5 minutes.

Flip the meat over and generously brush with the root-beer glaze. Cook until just medium rare, about 2 minutes. Flip again, brush the meat side with the glaze, and remove to a cutting board. Let rest 5–8 minutes.

To serve, sprinkle with toasted sesame seeds, then slice across the grain.

▶ **DRINK PAIRING** Cognac, a staple in many duck sauces, is just as good in a glass. Try a Brandy Daisy: Combine 2 oz (60 ml) cognac, the juice from half a lemon, and a dash of grenadine in a shaker with ice, shake, then strain into an ice-filled glass. Top with sparkling water.

CRISPY SEARED PHEASANT BREASTS IN GIN CREAM

Owing to their small size, densely textured flesh, and inherent leanness, boneless gamebird breasts present a challenge. They're best cooked hot and fast—or low, slow, and wet in a braise or a stew. Or, as in this recipe, you can combine the two techniques in the same pan. The quick blast of the high-heat sauté crusts the breasts with a brown crackle, and the subsequent simmer in herb-infused cream ensures a juicy texture.

SERVES 4

1½ lb (750 g) boneless upland gamebird breasts

Salt and freshly ground black pepper

1 tablespoon olive oil

3 tablespoons finely chopped shallots or onion

¼ cup (2 fl oz/60 ml) gin

¾ cup (6 fl oz/180 ml) heavy cream

3 tablespoons chopped fresh marjoram

1 teaspoon freshly squeezed lemon juice

Season the breasts with salt and pepper. You can leave the skin on or remove—whichever you prefer. Heat the oil in a skillet over high heat. Sear the breasts for about a minute per side, just enough to brown their exteriors and give them a slightly crisp edge. Remove them to a plate.

Reduce the heat to low, then add the shallots. Stir constantly for about a minute, until they are limp but not brown, then add the gin. Let it simmer for about 45 seconds. Add the cream and most but not all of the marjoram, bring it to a simmer, then return the breasts to the pan. Cover. After about 2 minutes, cut into the thickest part of a breast. Remove them when they still have some juicy pinkness in the center.

Let the cream mixture simmer until it's the consistency of a sauce, perhaps a minute longer. Add the remaining marjoram, the lemon juice, and salt and pepper to taste; stir. Ladle the sauce over the breasts and serve.

HOW TO COOK GAME LIKE YOUR GRANDDAD

Our grandparents didn't turn up their noses at some of the lesser creatures to wind up in a cooler. Maybe it's time we all threw an opossum on the grill if for no other reason than that's what we're missing. Here are a few ways to cook some critters that will broaden your culinary horizons.

OPOSSUM Ready to bring back this long-lost Southern staple? Season a cleaned opossum with salt and pepper; then dust it lightly with flour. Place it on its back in a roasting pan, add ½ cup water, and bake at 350°F (180°C) for one hour. Drain the water and arrange split sweet potatoes around the opossum. Sprinkle with a tablespoon of sugar, cover with 6 bacon slices, cook another 30 minutes, and enjoy.

MERGANSER Like liver, fish-eating duck meat is strong. So it only makes sense to treat merganser like liver: Marinate the breast fillets overnight in brandy, olive oil, garlic, and paprika. Fry them in bacon grease with onions. Eat, and don't expect it to taste like chicken.

GROUNDHOG What to do with the beloved pasture poodle? Noodle it. Parboil a cleaned groundhog and remove the meat. Cook 2½ cups of noodles in one can of beef broth and ½ cup water. Add 1 tablespoon cornstarch, a dash of salt and pepper, and 1 tablespoon butter. Mix together 1 cup of cooked peas and ½ cup onion. Dump it all in a casserole dish, top with french-fried onion rings, and cook 30 minutes at 350°F (180°C) for a dinner that will make a vengeful gardener's day. —T.E.N.

WINTER

The woods are stripped down to their bones, the gunpowder-colored sky threatens rather than invites, and the grim thermometer outside cautions us against foolishness. Still, we persist: we love the landscape even when it doesn't love us back. The northern hare hunters prowl the woods on snowshoes, their red faces chapped by the cold, while a tough-skinned subset of waterfowlers gravitates toward the open-water areas on partly-frozen lakes, in pursuit of late-season ducks. And when those lakes finally freeze, the ice fishermen emerge—some sitting in the open beside holes they've bored through the ice, bundled against the wind, while others tow shanties onto the flat whiteness. Sometimes the fish they catch are tossed through the shanty door, like drunks from an old-timey saloon, for quick and natural freezing. At camp and at home, it's a time for hauling in firewood, for stoking woodstoves until they're almost glowing orange, for the hot bosky bite of undiluted whiskey, for stews gurgling atop the stove in a cast-iron Dutch oven, for the stinging relief of searing one's frozen hands on a cup of camp coffee.

The deep-freeze is at its fullest now, and the simpler cooking of fall—those quick-roasted tenderloins, for instance—gives way to the more complex and slower-cooked dishes of deep winter, with low burner flames melting those more rugged cuts of meat into succulence.

For hunting and angling, as well as for cooking, winter presents a slew of challenges. But that roaring fire, the way that stew heats your ribcage, that scorching sip of whiskey, the bleached silent vista outside the icy-fingered window, the satisfaction of a harsh but heartening day afield: these are its enduring rewards, outweighing the challenges by far.

VENISON BACKSTRAP WITH RED PEARS & PICKLED GOLDEN RAISINS

Chef Paul Kahan of The Publican in Chicago knows his way around a backstrap. His favorite venison meal of all time was a backstrap he cooked on an old propane camp stove in an ice shanty by simply searing and basting it with lots of butter, maple syrup, and coarse black pepper. This is a more complex and refined take on that shanty meal, but the essence remains: a perfect combination of sweet, sour, and savory that might become your favorite venison meal.

SERVES 4

VENISON & MARINADE*
2 lb (1 kg) backstrap (venison loin), cleaned of all silverskin and cut into 2 even chunks

2 tablespoons extra-virgin olive oil

1 sprig fresh thyme

1 tablespoon coarse cracked black pepper

1 tablespoon grapeseed or canola oil

¼ cup (2 fl oz/60 ml) red wine

1 teaspoon red wine vinegar

¼ cup (2 fl oz/60 ml) beef or chicken stock

2 teaspoons butter

Salt and freshly ground black pepper

ROASTED PEARS
2 ripe red Anjou pears or other firm pears

2 teaspoons grapeseed or canola oil

2 teaspoons sugar

1 sprig rosemary (roughly 2 teaspoons fresh rosemary leaves)

PICKLED GOLDEN RAISINS*
2 tablespoons mustard seed

½ cup (3 oz/90 g) golden raisins

½ cup (4 fl oz/125 ml) white wine vinegar

¼ cup (2 fl oz/60 ml) maple syrup

*Venison may be marinated and raisins pickled 1 day ahead.

MAKE THE VENISON Marinate the venison in olive oil, thyme, and black pepper for at least 2 hours or up to overnight in the refrigerator.

Preheat the oven to 350°F (180°C). Heat a heavy-bottom ovenproof sauté pan over high heat until smoking hot. Add the grapeseed oil and sear the venison on all sides until golden brown. Place the pan in the oven. Roast until the internal temperature reaches 135°F (57°C) on an instant-read thermometer, 6–10 minutes. Remove the venison to a plate and let rest.

In the same pan, combine the red wine and the red wine vinegar. Reduce over high heat until thick and syrupy. Add the stock to the pan and reduce until syrupy again. Add the butter to the pan and whisk to combine. Taste and season with salt and pepper.

MAKE THE ROASTED PEARS Preheat the oven to 375°F (190°C). Core the pears and cut into eighths. Toss them in a bowl with oil and sugar to coat.

Toast the rosemary sprig in a dry sauté pan over medium heat until you hear a popping sound, being careful not to burn the leaves. Add the rosemary to the pears, salt and pepper to taste, and toss briefly. In an ovenproof pan, bake until tender and golden, 25–35 minutes.

MAKE THE PICKLED GOLDEN RAISINS Put the mustard seeds in a dry skillet over medium heat and shake occasionally until they start to pop. Remove from the heat. Let the mustard seeds cool in the pan, shaking gently every minute or so, until toasted and fragrant.

Put the raisins in a heatproof container. In a small sauté pan, combine the vinegar, ¼ cup (2 fl oz/60 ml) water, the syrup, and the toasted mustard seeds. Bring to a boil, stirring to prevent burning. Pour the hot vinegar mixture over the raisins. Let cool. (Cover and refrigerate if making ahead.)

▶ **SERVING TIP** Cut the venison on an angle and arrange on a plate. Nestle the pears alongside. Sprinkle with raisins and drizzle sauce on top. —C.K.

WILD GAME RAVIOLI

Fill these ravioli with whatever you have on hand—venison, small game, upland birds, or waterfowl. Just be sure that it's ground finely enough that you can seal the pasta around it.

SERVES 8

2 tablespoons olive oil

½ lb (8 oz/250 g) wild game, ground or very finely chopped

2 green onions, finely chopped

1 egg, lightly beaten

¼ cup (1 oz/30 g) grated Parmesan cheese, plus more for garnish

Salt and freshly ground black pepper

Cornstarch for dusting

24 wonton wrappers

½ lb (2 sticks/250 g) unsalted butter

16 fresh sage leaves, chopped

In a large skillet, heat the olive oil over medium heat and add the meat and green onions. Cook, stirring often, until the meat is browned, then set it aside to cool in a large bowl. Mix in the egg and cheese, and season with salt and pepper.

Dust a sheet pan or pans with cornstarch to prevent sticking and lay the wonton squares on the pan(s). Working swiftly, place a tablespoon or so of the meat filling on the center of each square. (You may need to adjust the amount of filling to keep the edges clear.) Using your fingers or a pastry brush, wet the edges of the squares with water, then fold them to form triangle shapes. Press the edges together tightly to form a solid seal. Put the ravioli in the refrigerator or freezer until ready to cook.

Bring a large pot of salted water to a boil. While it's heating, melt the butter in a large sauté pan over high heat. When the foaming subsides, lower the heat to medium and add the sage, and cook until the butter browns. Remove from the heat.

When the water is boiling, reduce the heat to medium-high and add the ravioli. Cook them until they float, about 3 minutes. Transfer them to the pan with the browned butter and gently toss for about a minute.

▶ **SERVING TIP** Spoon the ravioli with some butter into a pasta bowl and top with grated Parmesan to taste—and maybe a sage leaf.

BRAISED RABBIT WITH ROSEMARY & NIÇOISE OLIVES

Marco Canora, whose Italian-inflected cooking at New York's Hearth restaurant has earned him a bevy of awards and critical raves, has a simple but devastatingly good way to cook rabbit—seared, then bathed in a sauce of red wine, olives, and rosemary. It's equally delicious with ducks.

SERVES 4

2 rabbits, cut into 10 pieces each

Salt and freshly ground black pepper

About 7 tablespoons (3½ fl oz/ 100 ml) olive oil

1 cup (8 fl oz/250 ml) dry red wine

1 yellow onion, peeled and minced

1 carrot, peeled and minced

1 rib celery, minced

2 tablespoons tomato paste

3 or 4 rosemary sprigs, tied together with kitchen twine

About 5 cups (40 fl oz/1.25 l) chicken stock

½ cup (2.5 oz/75 g) Niçoise olives, pitted if desired

Preheat the oven to 325°F (165°C). Salt and pepper the rabbit. Heat 2 tablespoons of the olive oil in a large ovenproof sauté pan over medium-high heat. Add the rabbit in batches, to avoid crowding, and sear on both sides until nicely browned. Add another tablespoon oil for the second batch, if needed, and reduce the heat if it starts to burn. When finished, set the pieces of browned rabbit aside.

Pour the wine into the pan, raise the heat to high, and scrape the pan bottom with a wooden spoon to loosen the tasty brown bits. Reduce the heat and let the wine simmer for about 2 minutes, then pour it onto the reserved rabbit. Wipe out the pan.

Heat the remaining 4 tablespoons oil over medium-high heat. Add the veggies and sauté until softened, about 8 minutes. Add the tomato paste and rosemary. Stirring frequently, cook until the paste begins to darken, about 5 more minutes.

Return the rabbit to the pan, along with the wine and any accumulated juices. Cook for about 5 minutes, stirring, then add enough stock to come about halfway up the sides of the rabbit pieces, and bring to a boil. Add the olives, then cover, transfer the pan to the oven, and cook until the rabbit is falling-off-the-bone tender, about 1 hour. Remove the rosemary sprigs, season with salt and pepper, and serve.

FIELD DRESSING SMALL GAME

Once you've dressed your bag of squirrels and rabbits, getting them ready for the grill or pot is just a matter of removing the skin. And that process will go superfast if you follow these simple instructions.

THE SQUIRREL STRIP

1 Place the squirrel on the ground, stomach down. Pull the tail upward and cut through the tailbone from the rear, but do not cut through the hide on the top side. Leave that attached. Still pulling upward on the tail, use your knife to loosen the skin under the tail a bit.

2 Step on the tail, getting part of your foot onto the loosened skin. Then pull on the back legs, peeling the skin down. Pull the front feet out. Hook two fingers under the remaining skin on each thigh and remove it, pulling upward. Lop off the feet and head with a cleaver. —D.H.

THE RABBIT REVERSE

1 Remove the back feet above the ankles and the front legs above the knees with a cleaver. Using a sharp knife, slice under the skin along the back a few inches. Pull the skin away from the spine, creating a hand-size opening. Reach in, grab your naked bunny by the waist, and turn the skin inside out, pulling the skin down to the base of the head.

2 Using the cleaver, remove the head. If you didn't remove the tail when field dressing, split the pelvic bone with your knife, and cut into the base of the tailbone at a 45-degree angle on both sides to loosen it. Then pull towards the midsection, removing the tailbone and any remaining entrails. —D.H.

THREE WAYS TO MAKE YOUR MEAT LAST
Your game is now heaped on the countertop in small mountains of meat. Here's how to keep the meat fresh-as-the-day-it-was-killed if you plan to eat it within the following timeframes:

ONE WEEK Avoid the freezer—there's no need to risk freezer burn for such a short time period. Keep the meat unfrozen, well wrapped, and in the coldest part of the refrigerator, far away from the door.

ONE MONTH Center the meat in laminated freezer paper, fold the short ends over the meat, and turn the package over by rolling it along the counter edge. That will help move air out of the package. Once it's flipped, use your fingers to press the air out of the sides as if you're sealing an envelope. Repeat twice more and tape the flap.

ONE YEAR There's an easy and effective method for keeping meat edible for the long stretch. Use a vacuum sealer to suck all the air out of packages—it will stave off freezer burn and save freezer space. —T.E.N.

WILD GAME MINCEMEAT COBBLER

You rarely think of dessert when you're cleaning your deer. But here is dessert for the seriously devoted carnivore. Ground or very finely chopped game gets stewed with apples, raisins, dried cherries, spices, and a few splashes of dark rum, then baked under a sweet and golden cornmeal crust.

SERVES 10

FILLING

2 cups (16 fl oz/500 ml) apple cider or juice

1 cup (6 oz/185 g) dark seedless raisins

½ cup (3 oz/90 g) dried cherries or currants

1½ cups (6 oz/185 g) chopped peeled apples

1 teaspoon ground cinnamon

1 teaspoon ground cloves

1 teaspoon ground ginger

½ teaspoon salt

½ teaspoon ground nutmeg

¼ teaspoon ground allspice

¼ lb (125 g) ground or finely chopped wild game

CRUST

1 cup (5 oz/155 g) all-purpose flour, plus more for dusting

⅓ cup (2½ oz/75 g) cornmeal

3 tablespoons sugar

1½ teaspoons baking powder

½ teaspoon salt

5 tablespoons (2½ oz/75 g) cold unsalted butter, chopped

⅔ cup (5 fl oz/160 ml) heavy cream, plus 2 tablespoons

3 tablespoons dark rum or brandy (optional)

MAKE THE FILLING In a heavy saucepan, combine the cider, raisins, and cherries. Bring to a boil over high heat, then reduce the heat to low and simmer, covered, for about 30 minutes. Add the apples, spices, and game. Simmer for 2 hours more, adding more cider or water as needed to keep the mixture from sticking. Set aside to cool.

MAKE THE CRUST In a large mixing bowl, whisk together the flour, cornmeal, 2 tablespoons of the sugar, baking powder, and salt. Quickly work in the butter with your fingers until the mixture resembles coarse crumbs. With a spatula or wooden spoon, mix in ⅔ cup of the cream until the dough comes together just enough to be rolled into a ball. Knead it gently 2 or 3 times, then dust it with a bit of flour and place it on a floured surface. Roll it or pat it out so that it approximates the shape of the pan you'll be cooking in (e.g. a glass pie dish or a square baking pan).

BAKE THE COBBLER Preheat the oven to 350°F (180°C). Spoon the mincemeat mixture into the cobbler pan and, if using, splash with the rum. You can cut or tear the dough into pieces of any size or shape for the crust, cobbling them together, or place the dough whole atop the mincemeat (if the latter, poke a few holes in it with a knife to vent steam). Lightly brush the top of the dough with the remaining 2 tablespoons of cream, and sprinkle on the remaining tablespoon of sugar. Bake until the crust is golden and the filling is bubbling, 45–50 minutes.

▶ **SERVING TIP** Let cool for at least 15 minutes before serving, then top the warm cobbler with vanilla ice cream.

ROASTED GROUSE WITH MUSHROOMS & BACON

Ask any deer camp old-timer for a foolproof recipe, and you're likely to encounter a lot of canned cream of mushroom soup. There is a reason for that: Mushrooms plus cream plus meat equals a perfect trinity of flavors. This recipe chucks the can, with all its high-sodium gloppiness, while retaining that warm, earthy comfort that has made mushrooms and cream the go-to sauce for so many generations of hunters.

SERVES 4

GROUSE

4 grouse

4 tablespoons (2 oz/60 g) butter, softened

Salt and freshly ground black pepper

8 slices bacon

SAUCE

2 tablespoons butter

1¼ lb (625 g) cremini or wild mushrooms*, trimmed and thinly sliced

1 shallot, minced

1 cup (8 fl oz/250 ml) rich chicken stock (or defatted drippings from the pan)

3 sprigs thyme

½ cup (4 fl oz/125 ml) cream or crème fraîche

1 tablespoon bourbon

1 tablespoon fresh thyme leaves, chopped

*Morels, chanterelles, or a mix of wild and cultivated mushrooms all work well.

ROAST THE GROUSE Preheat the oven to 425°F (220°C). Rinse the birds, pat dry, then smear each with a tablespoon of softened butter. Generously salt and pepper, inside and out. Wrap 2 bacon slices around each grouse, then set them in a roasting pan. Roast in the oven until the grouse are browned, about 25 minutes. Remove to a plate and let rest, covered loosely in tinfoil, while you make the sauce.

MAKE THE SAUCE Melt 2 tablespoons butter in a large sauté pan over medium-high heat. Add the mushrooms and about ½ teaspoon salt, and sauté, stirring frequently, until the mushrooms release a lot of moisture and begin to smell fragrant, about 5 minutes. Reduce the heat to medium and add the shallot. Sauté until it is soft and most of the moisture has gone out of the pan, about 4 minutes. Add the stock and thyme sprigs, and simmer until the liquid is reduced by half. Pour in the cream and bourbon, and simmer until the sauce thickens, 3–5 minutes.

▶ **SERVING TIP** Spoon the sauce onto serving plates, and rest a grouse in the center of each. Sprinkle the thyme over top.

THE CANADIAN WHISKEY COMEBACK

For whatever reason, I encounter Canadian whiskey at hunting camps way more often than I encounter it in restaurants, bars, or homes. The reason? Could be the lower price. Could be the ultra-mellow (some would say watered-down) character, which lends itself to long hours of fireside sipping. Or it could just be tradition—the popularity of Canadian whiskey boomed during and after Prohibition, and as those of us who frequent family hunting camps are aware, Grandpa's way is often the only way.

Problem is, the quality of Canadian whiskey has remained level—that is to say, mostly mediocre—while in recent years American whiskey has undergone a massive and much-ballyhooed renaissance.

But there's good news—that imbalance is changing, with north-of-the-border distillers taking great strides to reinvigorate the category.

The folks behind Buffalo Trace, one of the sacred names in bourbon, are pioneering this revival with the release of Caribou Crossing and Royal Canadian Small Batch, two excellent examples of Canada's single-barrel comeback attempt—whiskeys with lots of rye spice and none of the old blandness. Forty Creek Whisky's Barrel Select, from Ontario, is barreled in old sherry casks, giving it a rich, distinct flavor. And for celebrating that trophy buck, there's Hirsch Selection's 20-year-old Canadian Rye Whiskey, from Nova Scotia, which is characteristically light yet intense and complex, a perfect sipping whiskey that'll bring a smile to any face, Grandpa's included.

ESSENTIAL SALTS

No tool or ingredient in your kitchen is more useful or versatile than salt. It preserves, pickles, cures, colors, encrusts, and heightens flavor. But as you're about to see, not all salts are created equal.

CURING Recipes for cured meats usually call for a touch of pink curing salt to kill bacteria and enhance preservation. It's not edible, and is dyed pink to prevent confusion with table salt.

KOSHER This should be your go-to cooking salt—especially with recipes that call for a salt crust. The coarse-grained flakes are easier to handle and stick to food better than table salt.

PICKLING Unlike table salt, pickling salt is free of the additives that would turn pickled vegetables dark and leave pickling brines cloudy.

FLEUR DE SEL Here we have the "flower of salt," the finest, whitest crystals on earth. Reserve this as the finishing touch for special meals only.

SEL GRIS Extra coarse and super moist, this gray sea salt from France can be used for cooking and finishing.

BLACK LAVA This is a specialty salt and has a strong flavor. Finish fish with it—or use it on salt-rimmed cocktails to give the drink a gunpowder-like touch.

DUCK PROSCIUTTO

Sounds fancy, but this is one of the simplest and most ancient tricks you can do with a piece of meat: Salt it for a couple of days, let it hang for a while to cure, and then indulge yourself in the rich, concentrated flavors. The only serious effort this recipe requires is patience.

SERVES 4-6

¾ cup (6 oz/185 g) kosher salt

¼ cup (2 oz/60 g) dark brown sugar

6 juniper berries, crushed

1 tablespoon ground white pepper

½ teaspoon smoked paprika (optional)

1 duck or goose breast, with as much of the skin on as possible

Mix the salt, sugar, and spices together in a small bowl. Spread out a large sheet of plastic wrap and spread half the salt mixture in the center. Place the duck breast on the salt, skin side down, then cover the breast with what remains. Gently rub the mixture into the meat to coat evenly, then bring the plastic wrap up and over the meat, twisting the ends to form a tight seal. Refrigerate to cure for 2 days, flipping daily.

Unwrap the duck breast and rinse well in cold water. Thoroughly pat the breast dry, and allow to dry further by resting it on a cooling rack for about an hour.

Wrap the duck breast in cheesecloth, tying off the ends with twine. At this point the meat needs to hang for at least two weeks. The ideal hanging environment is about 50°F (10°C) and humid, but a refrigerator will suffice. Get creative for the hanging apparatus: An S hook will do the trick, looped through the cheesecloth and hung on a refrigerator rack. So will a fishing hook and some monofilament. The key is to hang the prosciutto so that it's not touching anything and has sufficient air around it.

The meat will be very firm when ready to eat, and will have lost 30 percent of its initial weight. (Weigh the breast before hanging if you want to track this.) Unwrap the prosciutto and slice as thinly as possible. Serve with crusty bread, cheese, olives, and melon.

HOW TO PACK THE PERFECT HUNTING LUNCH

The perfect duck hunting lunch is the perfect duck sandwich. I'm not talking about anything fancy here. You'll want a hunk of stout bread, a leaf or two of crisp lettuce, and a good pickle for a nice snap. Last, you'll need an easy-as-you-please grilled duck breast fillet. There is no higher calling for a square foot of plastic wrap—and no finer way to feast in a blind.

If I'm lucky, I keep a supply of grilled duck breasts on hand starting from the day after opening day until the season's end. It's a straightforward setup—the breasts get an overnight swim in Italian dressing, then they're butterflied and grilled rare.

You can go with whatever's your favorite kind of bread, but I like the thin, chewy crust of a ciabatta roll, which is sturdy enough to hold up well when smashed into a shell bag or a parka pocket. I'll dress the sandwich with a smear of sun-dried tomato spread, my mama's crunchy sweet pickles, and a slab of Romaine. And that's it.

Of course, I've dated around over the years. I've been known to make a manly duck salad—yes, there is such a thing—by chopping the meat coarsely and mixing it up with black pepper and a dab of steak sauce. I'll even step out for the occasional dalliance with teriyaki marinade and onions caramelized alongside the breasts on the grill.

But I always come back to the old standby, my absolute favorite lunch, held with wind-chapped, muddy hands. Every last bite reminds me of why I'm out there in the first place. —T.E.N.

Why should you eat what you kill? For a moment, let's dismiss the most obvious reasons. Forget the nutritional value of venison, which has higher protein and lower cholesterol levels than domesticated, grain-fattened beef and pork. And set aside the flavor, which is more substantial and interesting than anything you're going to buy at the grocery. And never mind the economic benefits of a passion that can reward a day's work with enough meat to feed you for a year. And set aside how properly stored venison allows you to relive the memories from a great season again and again around your family's dinner table.

What's left? The biggest reason of all—our rights as hunters. Every year, American outdoorsmen lose critical wildlife habitat, hunting privileges, and access to land due to the actions of a public that often views hunting as a pointless and frivolous sport. Responsible hunters battle these losses with their votes, wallets, and pens—all very important—but we shouldn't forget to use our forks, as well.

Through our eating habits and thorough preparation of game, hunters need to demonstrate to others that we count on wild places and animals for an important part of our physical sustenance. Recent national food discussions rely on terms that will look mighty familiar to hunters: *locally raised, locally harvested, free-range, sustainable, grass-fed, humanely slaughtered.* Some non-hunters will never understand the passion that pulls us into the woods every year, but many will sympathize with our passion for what we bring home.
—S.R.

ELK & TOASTED CHILE STEW

Since elk are so lean, cut the meat larger for this recipe than you would for beef, and keep the stew at the barest simmer. This will help keep the meat tender.

SERVES 6

4 dried ancho chiles, stemmed and seeded

4 dried guajillo chiles, stemmed and seeded

1 dried cascabel chile, stemmed and seeded (omit for less heat)

1½ cups (16 fl oz/500 ml) boiling water

Salt and freshly ground black pepper

2 lb (1 kg) elk or other venison stew meat, cut into 1½-inch (4-cm) cubes

3 tablespoons olive oil

1 large yellow onion, chopped

6 cloves garlic, chopped

3 bay leaves

1 tablespoon fresh thyme leaves

1 tablespoon dried Mexican oregano

1 tablespoon ground cumin

½ cup (4 fl oz/125 ml) apple cider vinegar

MASA DUMPLINGS
1½ cups (8 oz/250 g) masa harina

2 tablespoons lard

½ cup (¾ oz/20 g) chopped cilantro, for garnish

Lime wedges, for garnish

In a cast-iron skillet over medium heat, toast the chiles for about 2 minutes. Put them in a bowl, cover with the boiling water, and soak until softened, about 30 minutes. Dump the chiles and the soaking water into a blender, and purée.

Salt and pepper the meat well. In a large, deep Dutch oven, heat the oil on high heat until almost smoking. Add the meat and brown well, 6–8 minutes. Remove the meat with a slotted spoon and set aside. Reduce the heat to medium-low and add the onion; sauté for about 4 minutes, until just softened, then add the garlic and cook for 2 minutes more. Add 2½ qt (80 fl oz/2.5 l) water and scrape the bottom of the pot with a wooden spoon, dislodging any browned bits. Add the bay leaves, thyme, oregano, cumin, vinegar, chile purée, and meat. Bring to a simmer, cover, and cook 2–3 hours, or until the meat is very tender.

MAKE THE MASA DUMPLINGS Line a sheet pan with wax paper. Make the dumplings by combining the masa harina and 1⅓ cups (11 fl oz/345 ml) warm water in a bowl to form a smooth paste. Mix in the lard and 1 teaspoon salt. Divide the dough into balls slightly larger than gumballs and place on the prepared sheet pan. Indent each with your pinky to make a small bowl shape. Add the dumplings to the simmering stew and cook for about 10 minutes.

Ladle the stew into bowls and serve garnished with the cilantro and lime.

ROASTED GOOSE WITH CRANBERRY, OYSTER & CHESTNUT STUFFING

In this recipe, a wild-goose roasting technique is paired with a cornbread stuffing loaded with just about every traditional Christmas flavor save that of popcorn garland. Be diligent with your meat thermometer, testing the bird regularly (every 30 minutes for the first hour and a half, then every 10 minutes after that). Serve with maple-glazed sweet potatoes and some cider-braised greens, or whatever family tradition dictates, plus a first-rate pinot noir.

SERVES 4

BRINE

2 gallons (256 fl oz/8 l) water

1 cup (8 oz/250 g) salt

1 cup (1½ oz/40 g) black peppercorns

1 cup (7 oz/220 g) brown sugar

One 4–5 lb (2–2.5 kg) wild goose, dressed, well plucked, and cleaned

STUFFING

3 tablespoons butter

1 cup (4 oz/125 g) diced yellow onion

¾ cup (4 oz/125 g) diced celery

2 teaspoons minced garlic

1 teaspoon chopped fresh sage

½ teaspoon cayenne pepper

Kosher salt and freshly ground black pepper

1 dozen oysters, shucked and drained, liquor reserved

¼ cup (1 oz/30 g) chopped roasted chestnuts

¼ cup (1 oz/30 g) dried cranberries, soaked in warm water to plump

2 large eggs, lightly beaten

1–2 cups (8–16 fl oz/250–500 ml) buttermilk

4 cups (8 oz/250 g) stale crumbled cornbread

½ cup (4 fl oz/125 ml) bacon fat (or oil)

2–4 cups (16–32 fl oz/500 ml–1 l) chicken stock

BRINE THE GOOSE Prepare the brine 1 day ahead. Heat some of the water in a saucepan, add the salt, and stir to dissolve. Then combine the salted water with the remaining water, peppercorns, and brown sugar in a large pot. Submerge the goose in this brine and refrigerate overnight.

MAKE THE STUFFING Melt the butter in a large sauté pan over medium-high heat. Add the onion, celery, and garlic, and cook, stirring occasionally, until soft, about 4 minutes. Season with the sage, cayenne, and 1 teaspoon each salt and pepper. Remove from the heat and set aside. When cool, fold in the oysters, chestnuts, and plumped cranberries. In a mixing bowl, whisk together the eggs, oyster liquor, and 1 cup of the buttermilk, and pour this mixture over the crumbled cornbread. After the cornbread has absorbed the liquid, fold in the oyster mixture. Add more buttermilk if the stuffing seems perilously dry, but don't overmoisten it.

ROAST THE GOOSE Preheat the oven to 350°F (180°C). Remove the goose from the brine, pat dry, and sprinkle salt and pepper all over. Heat the bacon fat in a large sauté pan or Dutch oven over high heat. Sear the goose on all sides until the skin is seared and lightly golden, 2–3 minutes per side. Season again with salt and pepper, making sure to include the inside of the goose this time, and fill it with the stuffing. (If you have any left over, bake it in a greased pan or glass dish alongside the goose for 55 minutes.) Truss the goose's legs and place it, breast side down, on a roasting rack.

Pour stock into a large roasting pan until it comes ¼–½ inch (6–12 mm) up the sides. Lower the rack with the goose into the pan and roast just until a thermometer inserted in the thigh reaches 160°F (71°C), roughly 2 hours. Maintain the liquid level by adding more stock, if necessary. (If the goose skin begins to singe, cover it loosely with a tent of tinfoil.) Remove from the oven and let the goose rest, uncovered, 10–20 minutes. The center of the stuffing must reach 165°F (74°C); if it's not cooked thoroughly, transfer it to a pan and place it back in the oven until done.

CITRUS-GLAZED FISH WITH WORCESTERSHIRE-PECAN RICE

Chef Danny Trace of Houston devised this killer recipe for Gulf redfish, but any fish benefits from it. Use a sharp chef's knife to peel the citrus—slice off the ends of each piece of fruit, stand upright on a cut side, and slice away the colored peels and white pith, following the contour of the fruit. Then, use your knife to quarter the fruit, picking out any seeds, or cut between the membranes to release each segment.

SERVES 4

GLAZE

1 *each* blood orange, navel orange, and lemon, peeled, seeded, and quartered

2 tablespoons minced shallot

1½ cups (12 fl oz/375 ml) agave syrup or honey

1 cup (8 fl oz/250 ml) distilled white vinegar

½ cup (4 fl oz/125 ml) tequila

WORCESTERSHIRE-PECAN RICE

1 tablespoon unsalted butter

2 tablespoons minced garlic

¾ cup (3 oz/90 g) chopped onion

¾ cup (3½ oz/105 g) *each* chopped green bell pepper and red bell pepper

½ cup (4 fl oz/125 ml) Worcestershire sauce

2 cups (14 oz/440 g) long-grain rice

3 bay leaves

Salt and freshly ground black pepper

1½ cups (6 oz/185 g) pecan halves or pieces, lightly toasted

1 *each* blood orange, navel orange, and lemon, peeled and segmented

About 4 oz (125 g) baby arugula

12 cherry tomatoes, halved

About 3 tablespoons Steen's sugarcane vinegar (optional)

4 red snapper fillets (or other tender white fish), about 8 oz (250 g) each

2 tablespoons vegetable oil

MAKE THE GLAZE Combine the blood orange, navel orange, lemon, shallots, agave syrup, vinegar, and tequila in a saucepan and bring to a boil. Reduce the heat to low, and simmer until the mixture has reduced to a syrupy consistency, about 5 minutes. Remove from the heat and let cool. Transfer mixture to a blender or food processor, and pulse to purée the solids. Strain the mixture through a fine-mesh sieve and reserve.

MAKE THE RICE Put the butter in a medium saucepan over medium heat. Add the garlic, onion, and peppers, and sauté for about 2 minutes. Add the Worcestershire sauce and cook, stirring, for another minute. Add the rice, 3¾ cups (30 fl oz/940 ml) water, and the bay leaves along with generous dashes of salt and pepper. Stir once, just to incorporate, then bring to a boil and cook until the water level reaches the top of the rice. Do not stir, but shake the pot occasionally. When all the liquid has dissipated, cover the pot and allow the rice to steam for 5 minutes. Fluff with a fork, and then fold in the pecan pieces. Keep warm.

Combine the additional orange and lemon segments in a bowl with the arugula, cherry tomatoes, and Steen's vinegar (if using). Season with salt and pepper, and toss gently to combine.

Season the fish fillets with salt and pepper. Heat the oil in a large, wide skillet over medium-high heat. When the oil is hot but not smoking, add the fillets and cook for about 2 minutes per side, until just cooked through. Remove the fillets to a sheet pan or large plate and brush with the reserved citrus glaze.

▶ **SERVING TIP** Divide the rice among 4 plates. Place a fillet on each plate and garnish with the citrus-arugula salad. Drizzle a bit more of the citrus glaze over the salad and fish, and serve immediately.

CAVEMAN ROASTED LEG OF VENISON

Here's one for your inner Neanderthal: a whole roasted venison leg, just like Fred Flintstone would've cooked it. This is game cookery at its most primal and dramatic, and the results are a showpiece—which is good, as you'll need a crowd to help you eat it. Because the meat is only mildly doctored—with a classic wet rub of olive oil, thyme, rosemary, garlic, and juniper berries—and cooked in an unforgiving manner, the key to success here is a prime hunk of meat, ideally from a younger deer, field dressed impeccably, and aged if possible. Thumping your chest while gnawing the bones is optional.

MAKES 1 ROAST

¼ cup (2 fl oz/60 ml) olive oil,
or as needed

½ cup (¾ oz/20 g) fresh thyme leaves

8 cloves garlic, minced

¼ cup (2 oz/60 g) roughly chopped fresh rosemary

3 tablespoons juniper berries, crushed

¼ cup (2 oz/60 g) kosher salt

¼ cup (⅓ oz/10 g) cracked black peppercorns

1 bone-in whole venison hind leg
(12–15 lb/375–470 g)

3 tablespoons vegetable oil

4 cups (32 fl oz/1 l) game or beef stock

In a small bowl, combine the olive oil, thyme, garlic, rosemary, juniper berries, salt, and pepper until it resembles a coarse paste. (Add a little more olive oil, if needed, to make it goopy enough to spread.) Rub this mixture onto the venison, wrap in plastic wrap, and refrigerate overnight. Remove the leg from the refrigerator a couple of hours before cooking. It should be at room temperature when it goes into the oven.

Preheat the oven to 350°F (180°C). Drizzle the meat with the vegetable oil, patting it lightly with your fingers to coat evenly, and place the leg on a rack set in a large roasting pan. Roast, undisturbed, for 1 hour.

Heat the stock to a low simmer on the stove top. Turn the meat. Using a baster or ladle, baste the meat with about half of the hot stock, and roast for another hour. Set the stock aside and keep warm, reheating it to a simmer just as the next hour is up.

Turn the roast a second time, and repeat the basting with the remaining stock. After about 15 minutes, start checking the meat in its thickest part, away from bone, with an instant-read meat thermometer. The cooking time will depend on the size of the roast. Remove the roast when the thermometer reads 120°F (49°C) for rare, or 126°F (52°C) for medium-rare. (The meat will keep cooking a bit after it's removed from the oven.)

Remove the roast to a large cutting board and allow it to rest for about 20 minutes. Carve and serve.

VENISON OSSO BUCO WITH ISRAELI COUSCOUS

To butcher an "osso buco steak," start with the hind shanks, as they have the most meat. Leaving the meat on the bone, cut the shanks into two or three steaks, each about 2 inches (5 cm) thick. Then cook them the way New York chef John DeLucie does—braised slowly in wine to impart flavor and tenderize the venison.

SERVES 6

OSSO BUCO

Six 14-oz (440-g) venison osso buco steaks

Salt and freshly ground black pepper

¼ cup (1½ oz/45 g) all-purpose flour

2 tablespoons oil

2 carrots, peeled and chopped

2 ribs celery, chopped

1 yellow onion, chopped

2 cloves garlic, chopped

1 can (14 oz/440 g) peeled Italian tomatoes, drained

1 bay leaf

2 cups (16 fl oz/500 ml) red wine

2 cups (16 fl oz/500 ml) chicken or beef stock

1 tablespoon butter

ISRAELI COUSCOUS

2 cups (16 fl oz/500 ml) beef stock

1½ cups Israeli pearl couscous

2 tablespoons butter

½ cup (¾ oz/20 g) chopped Italian parsley

6 dried figs, quartered and soaked in brandy to plump

Whole fresh herbs (thyme, chives, rosemary) for garnish

MAKE THE OSSO BUCO Season the venison steaks with salt and pepper and dredge them in the flour. Heat a deep sauté pan or Dutch oven over medium-high heat, add the oil, and brown the steaks in batches to avoid crowding the pan. Add the carrots, celery, onion, and garlic to the pan. When the venison is brown on both sides, remove the meat and vegetables from the pan, and discard the excess oil.

Add the tomatoes to the pan and roast for 2–3 minutes. Return the venison and vegetables to the pan. Add the bay leaf and cover the meat with the wine and the stock. Bring to a boil, then reduce the heat to low and cover. Simmer gently until the meat is tender and starts to fall off the bone, about 2 hours.

Carefully remove the venison from the pot and arrange it in an ovenproof dish. Strain the vegetables out of the sauce (discard them), and finish the sauce by blending in the butter. Pour the sauce back around the meat and place in a low oven to keep warm.

MAKE THE ISRAELI COUSCOUS In a large pot over high heat, bring the stock to a boil. Add couscous and cook until it is tender and most of the liquid has been absorbed. Remove from heat, then add the butter and season with salt, pepper, and the chopped parsley. Add the plumped figs to the couscous and toss well. Serve couscous with the venison and sauce, topped with your fresh herbs of choice.

▶ **DRINK PAIRING** Rich and potent, cabernet sauvignon has long been the go-to varietal for big game. The 2008 Chateau Smith Cabernet adds subtlety to the mix, with lots of brawny elegance but also tenderloin-friendly nuance. —C.K.

BUTCHERING BIRDS

Do you pluck or breast? Most folks usually do one or the other, but there are times when one method works best. So here are the upsides of each, the basic procedures, and some handy tips. Now, do you roast or grill? We'll leave that one up to you.

THE PERFECT PLUCK
THE UPSIDES It looks pretty. You use the whole bird. Leaving the skin on, as with chicken, helps retain moisture in the meat during the cooking process.

WHEN NOT TO PLUCK Your bird is so full of holes it wouldn't be pretty anyway. You've shot an early-season bird with lots of stubborn pinfeathers. You're in a hurry.

THE PROCEDURE Pluck before you gut; this keeps the cavity cleaner. The sooner you pluck after the kill, the easier. You can wet pluck your birds (dunk first into a pot of 140°–160°F/60–71°C water until the wing feathers pull out easily) or wax birds. Both work great, but dry-plucking is a bit easier. That's why I dry-pluck. Wear latex gloves to help you hold on to the feathers. The few wispy feathers usually hanging on after dry-plucking can be singed off with a small torch.

BONUS TIP Wings are hard to pluck, so if you can handle a change from the classic whole-bird presentation, cut them off. Lift the wing upward and clip through the joint with shears. —D.H.

WAX OFF
1 Using shears, remove the wings and cut the lower legs at the knee. Wear latex gloves to help you hold on to the feathers. Grab them by the handful and rough-pluck, being careful not to rip the skin.

2 For each duck, place ¼ lb (125 g) paraffin wax and 1 gallon (128 fl oz/4 l) water, hot enough to melt the wax, in a metal bucket. Holding the duck by the neck, dip it in the water and wax. After it's coated, dunk the duck into a bucket of cold water.

3 Let it sit for 5 minutes. The wax will harden, allowing you to peel it off with the remaining feathers.

THE BASICS OF BREASTING
THE UPSIDES It's quick and easy. And let's face it, some legs taste like shoe leather.

WHEN NOT TO BREAST You've got time and want to do things up fancy. You've cleanly shot a big, fat, fully-plumed bird, and it'd be a shame not to whole-roast such an animal.

THE PROCEDURE Run the point of your knife under the skin above the breast for an inch or two. Stick your fingers in and pull the skin away. Make a long slice tight along the breastbone. Turn your knife on its side and lift the meat as you cut it free, close to the rib cage. Clip the wishbone with shears or just work your knife around it to remove one half of the breast. Repeat on the other side.

BONUS TIP If you like your duck breasts whole, try this technique: Cut the wings off, close to the body. Peel the skin away from the breast. Lift up the bottom of the breast to loosen it from the rib cage. Hook a finger under the top of the breast, hold the neck, and then pull down. —D.H.

THE UPLAND MANEUVER
There's a quick and simple way to dress your grouse, woodcock, and quail. And you don't even need a knife.

1 Place the gamebird on the ground on its back. The bird's head should face away from you. Step on the wings, getting your feet close to the body—right where the wing meets the rib cage. Then, grab the legs and lift straight up.

2 A slow and steady pull turns the bird inside out and removes all skin, feathers, head, and entrails—leaving only the breast meat and the wings. Twist the wings counterclockwise to remove, then wash the breast meat. —T.K.

DUCK SALMI

A salmi is an oldfangled, richly flavored game stew—often served, like chipped beef, over toast—that was a popular delicacy in the 1890s. This modern version is just as rich, and a luscious, soul-satisfying use for whole ducks.

SERVES 4–6

2 large ducks (mallard, pintail, gadwall) or 4 small ones (shoveler, wigeon, teal)

Salt and freshly ground black pepper

5 tablespoons butter, softened

2 tablespoons vegetable oil

3 yellow onions, chopped

1 large carrot, peeled and chopped

2 ribs celery, chopped

2 cloves garlic, chopped

1 tablespoon dried thyme

2 whole cloves

2 cups (16 fl oz/500 ml) chicken stock

1 cup (8 fl oz/250 ml) dry red wine

2 tablespoons all-purpose flour

4 oz (125 g) white mushrooms, sliced

⅓ cup (3 fl oz/80 ml) cognac, sherry, or Madeira

2 tablespoons chopped Italian parsley

Toasted slices of baguette or other crusty bread, buttered for serving

Preheat the oven to 450°F (230°C). Dry the ducks, inside and out, and salt and pepper generously. Spread 2 tablespoons of the softened butter over each bird and place the ducks, breast side down, in a shallow roasting pan. Roast until the meat is barely rare; it will finish cooking later. The cooking time will depend on size, but start checking as early as 8 or 10 minutes in. Feel free to cut into the meat to check, as you'll be hashing it all up soon anyway. Remove from the oven and let cool. When cool enough to handle, chop the meat into medium-size pieces, reserving the bones, skin, and trimmings.

Heat the oil in a large pot or Dutch oven over medium-high heat. Sauté the onions, carrot, and celery for about 5 minutes. Add the garlic, thyme, and cloves, along with more salt and pepper, and cook for another minute. Add the trimmings, bones, and skin, and cook, stirring, for an additional minute. Pour in the stock and wine, and bring to a boil. Reduce the heat to low and simmer, uncovered, for about 2 hours, or until the mixture is reduced to about 2 cups (16 fl oz/500 ml). Occasionally skim the fat from the surface. Strain the sauce, discarding the vegetables and trimmings, and return the sauce to a gentle simmer.

Melt 2 tablespoons of the butter in a small saucepan over medium heat, then add the flour. Stir or whisk constantly to make a thick and slightly beige roux, about 6 minutes. Ladle some of the sauce into the roux and whisk to combine, then add a little more. Add this roux-sauce mixture to the sauce, whisking until well incorporated. It should resemble a thin gravy. Simmer for about 15 minutes, or until the sauce has thickened.

Wipe out the small saucepan and, over medium-high heat, melt the remaining 1 tablespoon of butter. When it bubbles, stir in the mushrooms, and cook, stirring occasionally, until wilted and brown. Add the cognac and bring to a quick boil. (Be careful. If you tilt the pan, it may erupt in flames. That's okay, and actually quite preferable. Just don't singe your eyebrows.) Add the mushrooms to the sauce, along with the reserved meat. Let the mixture simmer until the duck is just heated through; the heat of the liquid will bring it to medium-rare. Stir in the parsley. Serve with the toasted bread, either on top, like chipped beef, or with the bread on the side for scooping and dipping.

HOMEMADE PICKLES

2 cups (16 fl oz/500 ml)
red wine vinegar

1 cup sugar

2 jalapeño chiles, halved
lengthwise

12 cloves garlic

1 cinnamon stick

½ teaspoon mustard seed

½ teaspoon coriander seed

1 bay leaf

3 whole cloves

3 whole black peppercorns

3 cucumbers, sliced ¼ inch
(6 mm) thick

2 red onions, thinly sliced

2 red bell peppers, thinly sliced

4 serrano chiles

To make a pickling liquid,
combine the vinegar, sugar,
jalapeños, 8 cloves of the
garlic, cinnamon, mustard
seed, coriander seed, bay leaf,
cloves, peppercorns, and 2
cups (16 fl oz/500 ml) water
in a medium saucepan. Bring
to a boil over medium-high
heat, and boil for 3 minutes.

Meanwhile, combine the
remaining ingredients in a
bowl. Pour the hot pickling
liquid over them. Refrigerate,
uncovered, for 24 hours.

BRAISED & BARBECUED VENISON RIBS WITH HOMEMADE PICKLES

Here's an amazing recipe for venison ribs that starts off so low and slow that you may want to start cooking the day before you plan to eat it.

SERVES 4

1 rack of venison ribs
(at least 8 bones), or, if
unavailable, 8 rib chops

2 carrots, roughly chopped

½ rib celery, roughly chopped

2 white onions, roughly
chopped

6 cloves garlic

1 jalapeño chile, split

2 tablespoons chili powder

1 teaspoon whole black
peppercorns

½ teaspoon dried thyme

½ teaspoon dried sage

½ teaspoon ground cinnamon

1 bay leaf

1 cup (8 fl oz/250 ml)
favorite barbecue sauce

Homemade Pickles (*left*)

Preheat the oven to 250°F (120°C). Distribute all the ingredients except the barbecue sauce in a large casserole or roasting pan and add enough water to just cover the meat. Cover the pan with a tight-fitting lid or aluminum foil; or, even better, cover with both foil and a lid. Put in the oven and braise until the ribs are very tender, as long as 8 hours.

Remove the ribs from the roasting pan and let cool in the refrigerator overnight. Discard the cooking liquid.

Slice the rack into individual ribs and let them come to room temperature. Light a medium-hot fire (375°F/190°C) in your grill and oil the grill grate. Grill the ribs just until heated through, 2–3 minutes per side. Brush on the barbecue sauce and continue to cook, turning frequently, until they're browned but not blackened.

▶ **SERVING TIP** Serve the ribs with the homemade pickles and plenty of napkins.

VENISON NACHOS—CARNITAS STYLE

Carnitas, one of the true glories of Mexican cuisine, are traditionally made by braising richly marbled pork shoulder in its own fat, with a blast of spices and chiles adding even more flavor. Venison gets the same treatment here, with lard (or olive oil) lending to the richness. For added indulgence, the crispy-edged venison is strewn over tortilla chips and topped with bubbling cheddar for a wild version of nachos. The meat makes an incredible filling for tacos as well.

SERVES AT LEAST 6

About 2 lb (1 kg) venison roast, trimmed and cut into substantial chunks (1½ inch or so)

Salt and freshly ground black pepper

3 tablespoons olive oil

6 cloves garlic, roughly chopped

1 tablespoon juniper berries

2 tablespoons ground cumin

2 tablespoons oregano

4 bay leaves

2 canned chipotle chiles in adobo sauce, roughly chopped

1 qt (1 l) chicken stock

¼ cup (2 oz/60 g) lard (or olive oil)

Tortilla chips

8 oz (250 g) shredded sharp cheddar cheese

Limes, chopped cilantro, sour cream, guacamole, and/or pickled jalapeños for garnish

Pat the venison dry with paper towels, and season generously with salt and pepper. Heat the olive oil in a large pot or Dutch oven over medium-high heat. Add the venison in batches so as not to overcrowd the pan, and brown on all sides, about 12 minutes total. Transfer the browned pieces to a plate. Add the garlic to the pot and cook, stirring, for about 1 minute, then add the juniper berries, cumin, oregano, bay leaves, chipotles, and generous dashes of salt and pepper. Stir to combine, and cook for about 30 seconds more. Add the chicken stock along with the reserved venison and any accumulated juices on the plate. Bring to a simmer and cook, partly covered, for about 1½ to 2 hours, or until the venison is very tender but not quite falling apart. Remove the lid and continue to simmer for about 30 minutes more, until the liquid has almost evaporated.

Remove the venison with a slotted spoon, transferring to a plate. Discard any remaining liquid and solids, and clean and dry the pot. Return the pot to medium-high heat and add the lard. When it is hot, add the reserved venison pieces in batches and fry them until crispy. Transfer to a paper towel–lined plate, and, when cool enough to handle, shred the pieces.

Preheat the oven to 450°F (230°C). Arrange the tortilla chips on a sheet pan or, to make life easier, an ovenproof serving platter. Sprinkle the cheese over the chips, distributing evenly, then do the same with the shredded venison. Place in the oven and cook until the cheese has melted and the venison is sizzling.

Garnish as desired, and serve immediately.

GOOSE LEG SLIDERS

After slow-cooking for a few hours, this succulent meat makes a delicious slider with your condiment of choice, or you can mix it with your favorite barbecue sauce. Put some on a slider bun next to a crisp pickle chip, or whip up a quick slaw by whisking Dijon mustard, balsamic vinegar, sugar, and a little oil together and tossing it with shredded cabbage and carrots. Top your sliders and enjoy.

MAKES 1 PARTY'S WORTH OF SLIDERS

6–8 Canada goose legs

Salt and freshly ground black pepper

Cayenne pepper

3 tablespoons bacon grease

1 yellow onion, sliced

3 cloves garlic, mashed

½ cup (4 fl oz/125 ml) red wine

2 cups (16 fl oz/500 ml) stock (beef, or better yet goose or game), or as needed

Slider buns or other mini rolls for serving

Mayo, mustard, ketchup, or other favorite fixings

Preheat the oven to 250°F (120°C). Salt the goose legs liberally and sprinkle with a mix of black pepper and cayenne.

Heat the bacon grease in a sauté pan over medium-high heat. Brown the goose legs 1 or 2 at a time to avoid crowding. Transfer the browned legs to a roaster or Dutch oven, reserving the fat in the pan.

Sauté the onion and garlic in the skillet, adding a pinch of salt as they cook down. When the onions are translucent, deglaze the pan with a healthy dose of red wine. When the wine has reduced, pour this pan sauce over the goose legs.

Add enough stock to the roaster to come halfway up the level of the meat. Cover tightly with foil or a lid and place in the oven. Go hunting, or otherwise occupy yourself for several (2 to 4) hours.

Pull the roaster from the oven and remove the foil. The meat should be falling off the leg bones. If it's not, reseal the roaster, put it in the oven, and go back outside or watch a little pregame.

When the meat is ready, remove the bones from the pan and drain a bit of the liquid off. Use two forks to shred the meat into short strands. Toast your slider buns if you like, then top with meat and fixings. —D.D.

BRAISED SQUIRREL WITH BACON, FOREST MUSHROOMS & PINOT NOIR

Chef Levon Wallace of Louisville, Kentucky, on squirrel: "I'm not the most experienced hunter, but I did manage to bag a couple of grays this spring. I love the sweet aroma of squirrel, and I'm often surprised at most folks' inexperience with serving the little guys. A riff on coq au vin, this recipe works well for rabbit or duck, too. One decent-size squirrel will feed one person."

SERVES 4

4 squirrels, cleaned

1 bottle of pinot noir or other dry, light-bodied red wine

1 sprig thyme

1 sprig rosemary

4 bay leaves

1 tablespoon cracked juniper berries

1 teaspoon cracked black peppercorns

1 tablespoon brown sugar

Salt and freshly ground black pepper

2 cups (10 oz/315 g) all-purpose flour

3 slices thick-cut bacon, cut into 1-inch (2.5-cm) dice

1 cup (4 oz/125 g) pearl onions, peeled

2 cups forest mushrooms: shiitakes, morels, chanterelles, oysters, or your favorite variety

2 small carrots, diced

1 large rib celery, diced

1 clove garlic, smashed

Extra-virgin olive oil for drizzling

About ¼ cup (⅓ oz/10 g) chopped fresh Italian parsley

Remove the hind and forelegs from the squirrels with a pair of sharp kitchen shears. Trim the ribs away from the saddle and discard. Cut the saddle in half. You should now have six pieces per squirrel.

In a large nonaluminum bowl, combine half the bottle of wine (reserving the rest for braising the squirrel later) and the thyme, rosemary, 2 of the bay leaves, juniper berries, peppercorns, and brown sugar, stirring to dissolve the sugar. Add the squirrel pieces and marinate 6–8 hours or overnight, refrigerated.

Preheat the oven to 325°F (165°C). Remove the squirrel pieces from the marinade and pat dry with paper towels. Discard the marinade. Season the pieces with salt and pepper and dredge in the flour, shaking off any excess. Heat a Dutch oven or large, deep ovenproof skillet over medium-high heat. Add the bacon and cook until just crisp and golden brown. With a slotted spoon, transfer the bacon to paper towels to drain. Add the squirrel pieces (in batches if needed to avoid crowding) and brown them on both sides, about 4 minutes per side. Transfer to the plate with the bacon. Add the pearl onions and cook for about 3 minutes, or until golden brown, then add the mushrooms, carrots, celery, garlic, and remaining 2 bay leaves. Cook for another 3 minutes, stirring, until the vegetables are lightly caramelized. Add the remaining wine and bring to a boil, scraping the bottom of the pot to dislodge any tasty browned bits.

Return the squirrel and bacon to the pot, stir to incorporate, cover, and transfer the pot to the oven. Cook 1½–2 hours, or until the squirrel meat is tender but not falling off the bone. Serve immediately, drizzling with olive oil and sprinkling with parsley.

MOOSE STEW

Chef Marcus Samuelsson is best known for his wide-ranging and innovative cooking at Aquavit and Red Rooster. But Samuelsson grew up in Sweden, where moose is a mainstay. In this recipe, he incorporates a slew of eclectic influences into a satisfying moose stew. Try it with whitetails, too.

SERVES 6

3 tablespoons vegetable oil

3 lb (1.5 kg) moose (or deer, elk, or caribou) stew meat, cut into 1-inch (2.5-cm) cubes

Kosher salt and ground pepper

1 yellow onion, sliced

1 tablespoon curry powder

2 bay leaves

2 juniper berries

2 cups (16 fl oz/500 ml) chicken stock

1 cup (8 fl oz/250 ml) cream

½ cup (4 fl oz/125 ml) *each* cider vinegar, sherry, and port

1 carrot, roughly chopped

1 parsnip, roughly chopped

2 tablespoons mascarpone cheese

6 slices bacon, finely diced

2 tablespoons roughly chopped peanuts

1 cup (4 oz/125 g) jarred or frozen peeled pearl onions

1 tablespoon honey

2 apples, cored and cut into slices ⅛ inch (3 mm) thick

1 cup (2 oz/60 g) shredded spinach

1 tablespoon *each* grated fresh horseradish and coarsely chopped fresh Italian parsley, for garnish

Heat the oil in a large pot or Dutch oven over high heat. Season the moose with salt and pepper. Sauté the moose, onion, and ½ tablespoon of the curry powder until golden, about 8 minutes. Add the bay leaves, juniper berries, and 1 qt (1 l) water. Season with salt and pepper, and bring to a simmer; cook for 40 minutes.

Pour in the stock, cream, vinegar, sherry, port, and an additional 1 cup (8 fl oz/250 ml) water. Simmer for 20 minutes, then add the carrot and parsnip, and simmer again until tender, about another 20 minutes. Stir in the cheese.

While the stew is cooking, place the bacon in a large sauté pan over low heat. Cook until crispy, about 10 minutes. Drain the grease from the pan, leaving 2 tablespoons. Add the peanuts and the remaining ½ tablespoon curry powder, and sauté until the peanuts are toasted, about 2 minutes. Add the pearl onions and sauté for another 5 minutes, then add the honey and apples, and stir to coat. Cook for another 3 minutes. Add the spinach and cook until wilted, about 2 minutes. Season to taste with salt and pepper. Stir this mixture in with the stew just before serving.

▶ **SERVING TIP** Garnish with horseradish and parsley and serve.

---

5 EASY ANTELOPE MEALS

Pronghorn antelope is some of the best wild game you'll ever enjoy, and one of the most versatile.

SMOKY GRILLED BACKSTRAPS
Quick, simple, and so delicious: Cut a whole backstrap crosswise in thirds, dust with salt and pepper, and grill over a two-stage fire. Sear the pieces quickly on the hot side, then move them to the cool side of the grill to finish cooking. Add some hickory and applewood chunks to the coals for a touch of smoke.

GREEN CHILI Years ago, I came across a recipe that called for both antelope and hominy. It's now a staple at my house when I'm lucky enough to kill an antelope. Any green chili recipe will do—just substitute antelope for the pork.

BREAKFAST SAUSAGE Antelope lends itself really well to breakfast sausage. Your local butcher should sell you a pack of his premade seasoning, which is tough to beat. Otherwise, mix up your own blend with sage, thyme, rosemary, red pepper flakes, and brown sugar.

SATAY Meat on a stick offers near-endless possibilities and is a great way to use cuts normally reserved for roasts or round steak. Just about any marinade will do, especially something with lots of garlic and chiles. Serve the cooked and skewered meat pinched in a piece of flatbread with creamy *tzatziki*.

FAJITAS A great use for those random chunks left over from butchering is in fajitas. Braise the meat for a few hours with a red chili sauce, then serve them with onions and peppers sautéed separately.
—D.D.

VENISON CASSOULET

A wintry, bread-crumb crusted stew thick with meat, sausages, and white beans, cassoulet is often called the national dish of France. But don't let that intimidate you. It's really just beanie-weenies with an accent. This dish is also excellent with wild boar instead of venison.

SERVES 8

1 lb (500 g) dried white beans, soaked for at least 4 hours, or overnight, and drained

2 ham hocks

10 cups (80 fl oz/2.5 l) chicken stock

1½ cups (6 oz/185 g) chopped yellow onion

1 tablespoon minced garlic, plus 1 teaspoon

2 tablespoons chopped fresh thyme

2 bay leaves

1½ lb (750 g) boneless venison, cut into ½-inch (12-mm) cubes

Salt and freshly ground black pepper

½ cup (2½ oz/75 g) all-purpose flour

¼ cup (2 fl oz/60 ml) vegetable oil, or as needed

½ cup (2.5 oz/75 g) chopped celery

½ cup (2.5 oz/75 g) chopped carrot

¼ teaspoon cayenne

1 lb (500 g) smoked sausage, cut into 1-inch (2.5-cm) pieces

2 cups (8 oz/250 g) fine dried bread crumbs

8 tablespoons (1 stick/4 oz/125 g) unsalted butter, melted

¼ cup (1 oz/30 g) freshly grated Parmesan cheese

2 egg yolks

In a large, heavy pot, combine the beans and ham hocks with 8 cups (64 fl oz/2 l) of the chicken stock, ½ cup (2 oz/60 g) of the onion, 1 tablespoon minced garlic, 1 tablespoon of the thyme, and the bay leaves. Bring to a boil, then reduce the heat to low and simmer, uncovered, until the beans are tender, 45 minutes to an hour. Skim off any foam that floats to the surface. Drain, reserving the cooking liquid, and discard the bay leaves. When it's cool enough to handle, cut up the meat from the ham hocks and set it aside with the beans.

Preheat the oven to 375°F (190°C). Season the venison with salt and pepper, and dredge in the flour, shaking off any excess. Reserve the flour. Heat the oil in a heavy pot or Dutch oven over medium-high heat, and brown the venison on all sides, about 5 minutes total. (You may need to do this in batches to avoid overcrowding the pan.) Transfer it to paper towels to drain and cool.

In the same pot, adding a little more oil if needed, cook the remaining onion and thyme with the celery, carrot, ½ teaspoon salt, and the cayenne until the vegetables soften, about 4 minutes. Add the sausage and 1 teaspoon garlic to the pot and cook for 2 minutes, giving it an occasional stir. Now add ¼ cup (1½ oz/45 g) of the reserved flour and stir constantly, for about 10 minutes, until the flour darkens to a butterscotch color. Whisk in the remaining 2 cups chicken stock and the reserved cooking liquid from the beans. Bring to a simmer and cook for 15 minutes. Stir in the venison, the reserved meat from the ham hocks, and the beans. (At this point you can refrigerate it overnight if desired. Let it stand at room temperature for 30 minutes before baking.)

In a blender, pulse the bread crumbs, melted butter, cheese, egg yolks, and a generous sprinkling of salt and pepper until well blended. Spread this mixture over the cassoulet and bake until the crust is golden, about 35 minutes. Serve.

▶ **DRINK PAIRING** The national dish of France deserves to be married to a first-rate French wine. Try a hearty red from the southern Languedoc region, the same area where cassoulet originated.

A BRIEF HISTORY OF CHILI

Of all the myriad theories about the origins of chili, my favorite comes from George Leonard Herter, whom old-timers might remember as the bombastic voice of the Herter's catalog, a primary source for mail-order hunting gear in the '50s and '60s. Herter authored a slew of outdoor books, but his classic volume, self-published in 1960, was *Bull Cook and Authentic Historical Recipes and Practices*. Its opening lines neatly convey the book's harum-scarum breadth: "For your convenience I will start with meats, fish, eggs, soups and sauces, sandwiches, vegetables, the art of French frying, desserts, how to dress game, how to properly sharpen a knife, how to make wines and beer, how to make French soap and also what to do in case of hydrogen or cobalt bomb attacks, keeping as much in alphabetical order as possible."

Herter stuffed *Bull Cook* with all manner of deliciously crackpot theories and declarations ("I am the first man who ever made a hamburger in Africa"), including his history of chili. Chili, Herter decreed, was invented by Saint Mary of Agreda, a 17th-century Spanish nun said to have appeared, via teleportation, in the deserts of the American Southwest. During one of those visits, according to Herter, she bestowed a recipe upon the Native American tribes that called for venison, chile pepper pulp, tomatoes, and various other ingredients to be stewed together. Thus was chili born. I'm fond of this theory for two reasons—it puts venison, not beef, in the inaugural pot, and I like the idea of chili being a product of "intelligent design," as they say. After a bitterly cold afternoon in the deer stand, it's hard to imagine that a steaming red bowl of venison chili could be anything but heaven-sent.

Herter's imagination notwithstanding, his "original" chili recipe is an excellent one—it's based on a two-to-one mixture of venison and pork (though the original, he notes, called for javelina), the pork lending flavorful fat to the chili and tamping down any gaminess—and provides a fine jumping-off point for discussing the finer points of chili-making. Of course, such discussions—whether beans have any place in chili, cubed meat versus ground, etc.—often lead to arguments. Over the last century and a half, those arguments have resulted in untold barroom brawls, an Oklahoma prison riot, a Louisiana duel, red-hot rhetoric on the U.S. Senate floor (in 1983, New Mexico's Pete Domenici denounced Texan and Oklahoman chili as an "inedible mixture of watery tomato soup, dried gristle, half-cooked kidney beans, and a myriad of silly ingredients that is passed off as food"), and the 1979 divorce of an Arkansas couple. So I'll try to tread gingerly here.

Let's start with the basics: The tender cuts don't belong in a chili pot. With its long wet cooking time and gut-punch of seasonings, chili is the ideal venue for tougher cuts—neck, shoulder, flank, brisket, shanks, and trimmings. Like Herter, I prefer cubed meat—it gives the chili a consistency more like stew, and lets the wild flavors shine more brightly—but I wouldn't duel or divorce over it. Adding pork is another great tack for the lean venison.

Using beans? Fine. But cook them separately, ladling the chili over the top to serve. They'll be more tender this way (the acid in tomatoes prevents beans from softening), and the beans' starches won't render the chili gluey, which is bad—but so is watery. The traditional thickener, *masa harina*, or corn flour, is the best, but use sparingly—too much can flatten out the flavors. If using fresh tomatoes, peel them by blanching them in boiling water for a minute and then rubbing off the skins. This quick maneuver prevents any skin strands from annoying the chili's texture.

Beyond that, it's every cook's own. One of the grander aspects of chili-making is the individualistic nature of the cooking—it's a culinary free-for-all. It's beside the point whether a divinely-inspired Mary of Agreda transmitted it telepathically, or whether it developed as a means of disguising the taste of overripe meat on the frontier. A hot, deep bowl of venison chili is as close to manna from heaven as you're likely to find in deer camp.

ULTIMATE CAMP CHILI

Nothing fancy here, not even a tomato—just the most rib-sticking, appetite-sating, down-home bowl of Texas red that you and your deer camp buddies have ever had. Serve hot and often.

2 lb (1 kg) venison, cut into ½-inch (12-mm) cubes

1 lb (500 g) pork shoulder, cut into ½-inch (12-mm) cubes

3 tablespoons all-purpose flour

Salt and freshly ground black pepper

¼ cup (2 fl oz/60 g) vegetable oil

4 cloves garlic, minced

6 tablespoons (½ oz/15 g) ancho chile powder

1 tablespoon dried oregano

1 teaspoon freshly ground cumin seeds

4–5 cups (32–40 fl oz/1–1.25 l) game or beef stock

1 tablespoon masa harina mixed with 2 tablespoons water

Cayenne pepper (optional)

4 cups (28 oz/875 g) cooked pinto beans (optional; if using canned, drain and rinse well)

Lime wedges for serving

Combine the meats in a bowl and sprinkle with the flour, salt, and pepper; stir until evenly coated. In a large pot or Dutch oven, heat the oil over medium-high heat and add the meat. Cook, stirring frequently, until the meat is browned. Add the garlic and cook for 2 minutes. Add the chile powder, oregano, and cumin, and stir. Slowly mix in 4 cups (32 fl oz/1 l) of the stock.

Once it boils, reduce the heat to a simmer, and cook for 1½ hours, or until the venison is fork-tender. Add more stock as necessary to keep it from sticking or overthickening. Add the masa harina paste, stir well, and simmer for 10 more minutes. Add salt, pepper, and cayenne, if desired, to taste. If using beans, heat them now in a separate pot.

▶ **SERVING TIP** Ladle the beans into a bowl and top with the chili. Serve with lime wedges.

SERVES 6

MARY OF AGREDA'S CHILI CON CARNE DE VENADO

This is George Herter's rendering of the recipe. Buying his tale demands a bit of faith, but here's an indisputable fact: That nun (or Herter) had pretty good taste in chili. The version below was adapted from *Bull Cook and Authentic Historical Recipes and Practices*.

2 tablespoons lard or beef suet

1 medium onion, finely chopped

4 cloves garlic, finely chopped

2 lb (1 kg) venison, cut into ½-inch (12-mm) cubes

1 lb (500 g) pork shoulder, cut into ½-inch (12-mm) cubes

1 quart fresh ripe tomatoes, peeled and roughly chopped

1 cup chile pepper pulp, or 6 tablespoons (½ oz/15 g) chili powder mixed with 1 tablespoon flour

2 tablespoons fresh oregano

1 tablespoon salt

1 teaspoon cumin powder

3 bay leaves

2 cups cooked kidney beans (see note)

In a Dutch oven or large pot, heat the lard or suet over medium-high heat. Add the onions and cook until softened and beginning to brown; add the garlic and cook for 1 minute longer. (If using chili powder and flour rather than chile pulp, mix the two with enough cold water to make a paste, then stir into the onion mixture until smooth.)

Stir in the meat, and brown. Add the tomatoes and pulp and simmer for 20 minutes. Add the oregano, salt, cumin, and bay leaves and simmer, covered, for 2 hours. Check occasionally to make sure the chili isn't drying out; add water as necessary, but not too much.

▶ **NOTE** Herter's method: Soak dried beans overnight in water. Drain, then mix with ⅓ pound salt pork, a pinch of oregano, and fresh water to cover. Simmer at least 2 hours until beans are tender, drain, and serve chili over top.

SERVES 6–8

CHRISTMAS (BEER-CAN) GOOSE

Most backyard chefs are familiar with beer-can chicken, the technique for grilling a whole bird atop an opened can of beer. Here, we put it to use with a wild goose, replacing the grill with an oven and the beer with a blend of red wine and spices that infuses the bird with holiday spirit.

SERVES 4

RUB
Zest of 2 lemons

Zest of 2 limes

3 teaspoons paprika

1 teaspoon dried thyme

1 teaspoon ground sage

4 teaspoons kosher salt

2 teaspoons freshly ground back pepper

GOOSE
1 whole wild goose (about 7–10 lb/3.5–5 kg)

4 tablespoons (2 fl oz/ 60 ml) melted butter

1 can (32 oz/1 l) lager beer

2 cups (16 fl oz/500 ml) red wine

2 tablespoons balsamic vinegar

1 tablespoon Worcestershire sauce

4 cloves garlic, minced

2 cloves

1 cinnamon stick (or 2 teaspoons ground cinnamon)

MAKE THE RUB Combine the rub ingredients in a small bowl. Dash a quarter of the rub into the goose's body cavity. Brush the skin with about half of the melted butter, then sprinkle another quarter of the rub all over the goose, rubbing it lightly into the skin.

MAKE THE GOOSE Open the beer with a can opener, removing the top completely, pour out the beer, and save for another use (I'm sure you'll think of something). Rinse out the can, pour the wine into the can, then add the vinegar, Worcestershire, garlic, cloves, cinnamon, and generous dashes of salt and pepper.

Remove all but the bottom rack from the oven, making room for the goose to stand upright without touching the oven's top. Preheat to 350°F (180°C). Place the beer can in a large roasting pan and lower the goose onto the can. Adjust the legs to form a tripod and stabilize the bird. Carefully place in the oven.

Every 20 minutes, baste the goose with the remaining butter and rub mixture. Remove from the oven when a meat thermometer inserted in the thickest part of the thigh (away from the bone) reads 160°F (71°C). Let rest, uncovered, 10–20 minutes. Carefully lift the goose from the can and transfer it to a platter. Carve and serve.

STEWED DUCK WITH APPLES & TURNIPS

If you're a regular at duck camp, this meal should become a staple. Save the leftovers for lunch—the duck is almost as delicious cold the next day as it is hot out of the pot.

SERVES 4–6

2 mallards, cut into 8 pieces

Salt and freshly ground black pepper

1 teaspoon Chinese five-spice powder

3 tablespoons all-purpose flour

1 tablespoon olive oil

2 yellow onions, diced

1 carrot, peeled and diced

1 celery root, peeled and diced

1 lb (500 g) turnips, peeled and diced

5 Fuji apples, cored and diced

4 cloves garlic, minced

1 qt (32 fl oz/1 l) chicken stock

2 teaspoons cider vinegar

2 teaspoons sugar

Season the duck pieces all over with salt, pepper, and five-spice powder. Dust lightly with flour.

In a large pot or Dutch oven, heat the olive oil over medium-high heat. Add the duck and brown all over, 2–3 minutes per side. When the skin is crisp, remove the duck to a plate, reserving the fat in the pot.

Add the onions, carrot, celery root, turnips, apples, and garlic to the pot with the rendered duck fat and lower the heat to medium. You just want to soften the vegetables at this point, about 5–7 minutes; you're not looking to brown them.

Add the chicken stock, cider vinegar, and sugar. Bring to a boil. Return the duck legs to the pot, cover, reduce the heat to low, and simmer slowly for about 1 hour.

Now, feel free to go join the folks in the other room and brag about that nice deer you shot today.

When the hour's up, add the duck breasts and cook 15–30 minutes more, until the duck meat is fork-tender. Try serving with Louisiana brown jasmine rice. This is a Southern dish, after all.

▶ **DRINK PAIRING** A saison, or farmhouse ale, has the earthiness to go with fowl and enough carbonation to cut the richness. —C.K.

HOW TO COOK (ALMOST) ANY DUCK

Shooting a limit of ducks feels great, but coming home with a mixed bag can be just as exciting—at least once you get in the kitchen. The flavors (and cooking times) of these rich gamebirds vary greatly, giving you the chance to test and enjoy some new recipes.

SPECIES Teal
TYPICAL SIZE 1–1½ lb
FLAVOR PROFILE Mild and extremely tender
MAY WE SUGGEST Spicy Asian stir-fry

SPECIES Widgeon
TYPICAL SIZE 1½–2½ lb
FLAVOR PROFILE Subtle hints of iron, not unlike veal
MAY WE SUGGEST A hearty cassoulet

SPECIES Scaup
TYPICAL SIZE 1½–3 lb
FLAVOR PROFILE Briny and aggressive
MAY WE SUGGEST Gumbo

SPECIES Northern Shoveler
TYPICAL SIZE 2 lb
FLAVOR PROFILE Pronounced earthiness, almost vegetal
MAY WE SUGGEST Rustic duck sausage

SPECIES Mallard
TYPICAL SIZE 2–4 lb
FLAVOR PROFILE Savory and steak-like
MAY WE SUGGEST Grilled breasts

SPECIES Canvasback
TYPICAL SIZE 3–5 lb
FLAVOR PROFILE The "duckiest" duck; rich and flavorful
MAY WE SUGGEST Roasted whole
—D.D.

RABBIT SOTT'OLIO

Chef Craig Wallen, co-owner of New York City's Spasso restaurant, does an amazing thing with rabbit: Employing an age-old Italian method of preserving meats and vegetables called *sott'olio* [soh-TOL-yo], he submerges rabbits in oil and then slow-cooks them until the meat is beautifully tender and rich. He then dresses the warm meat in a salad of arugula, pickled onions, roasted carrots, and pine nuts for a perfect counterbalance. The only difficult part of this recipe is pouring that much oil into a pot—but it's worth it. And be sure to fish the garlic cloves out of the oil, save for later, and spread on toasted bread for a killer snack.

SERVES 4

2 whole wild rabbits, cleaned

Salt and freshly ground pepper

About 3 quarts (3 l) vegetable oil

About 1 quart (1 l) olive oil, plus 5 tablespoons (3 fl oz/80 ml)

2 whole heads garlic, broken into individual unpeeled cloves

6 sprigs fresh thyme

⅓ cup (3 fl oz/80 ml) red wine vinegar, plus ¼ cup (2 fl oz/60 ml)

1 red onion, sliced

2 carrots, peeled and chopped into ½-inch (12-mm) pieces

4 cups (2½ oz/75 g) baby arugula

¼ cup (1¼ oz/37 g) pine nuts, lightly toasted

¼ cup (1 oz/30 g) freshly shaved or grated Parmesan cheese

Preheat the oven to 300°F (150°C). Rub the rabbits with salt and pepper and place in a Dutch oven or other covered pot, or a high-sided roasting pan. Pour in a mixture of about 3 parts vegetable oil to 1 part olive oil, enough to fully submerge the rabbits. Add the garlic and thyme to the oil, and cover the pan as tightly as possible. (A sheet or 2 of aluminum foil underneath the lid is a good idea.) Place in the oven and cook for about 1½ hours, or until the meat is tender and falling off the bone. Let cool.

Meanwhile, combine ⅓ cup of the red wine vinegar in a small saucepan with ⅓ cup water, and bring to a boil over high heat. Place the red onion slices in a bowl, and pour the vinegar mixture over the onions. Stir, add salt and pepper, then allow the onions to pickle in this mixture at room temperature.

Heat 1 tablespoon of olive oil over low heat in a saucepan, and add the carrot pieces. Cook, stirring occasionally, until the carrots are tender but not mushy, 6–8 minutes. Salt and pepper to taste, and reserve.

Make a vinaigrette: In a small bowl, combine the remaining ¼ cup red wine vinegar with ¼ cup (2 fl oz/60 ml) olive oil and whisk thoroughly until the oil and vinegar are completely integrated. Season with salt and pepper.

When the rabbits are cool, remove the meat from the bones and reserve. To serve, reheat the rabbit meat in a small pan with some of the oil, over low heat, just to warm through. In a large mixing bowl, gently toss the arugula with the drained red onions, carrots, pine nuts, cheese, and about 3 tablespoons of the vinaigrette. Divide the salad among 4 plates, and top with the rabbit meat, adding a few more shavings of cheese and salt and pepper as desired.

ELK CARBONNADE

Carbonnade is a traditional, rib-sticking Belgian stew made with beef, onions, and a hearty spike of dark beer. Adapted here for elk, it's the perfect remedy for a cold day in the field, and a sly way to integrate the two primary hunting-camp food groups (those being meat and beer). Meat from whitetails, muleys, or moose will be equally good.

SERVES 6

2 tablespoons butter

4 slices bacon, chopped

3 lb (1.5 kg) elk or venison stew meat, cut into 2-inch (5-cm) cubes

Salt and freshly ground black pepper

3 yellow onions, chopped

1 tablespoon dark brown sugar

4 cloves garlic, minced

16 oz (500 ml) Belgian dark strong ale or other dark flavorful beer

1 cup (8 fl oz/250 ml) chicken stock, or as needed

1 bay leaf

1 teaspoon dried thyme

1 teaspoon apple cider vinegar or lemon juice

Cooked buttered egg noodles or dumplings for serving (optional)

¼ cup (⅓ oz/10 g) chopped parsley

Heat a large pot or Dutch oven over medium-high heat. Add the butter and bacon, and cook the bacon until barely crispy. Remove it with a slotted spoon, reserving the bacon for later and leaving the bacon grease in the pot. Pat the stew meat dry with paper towels, then salt and pepper generously. Add the stew meat to the pot in batches, to avoid overcrowding, and raise the heat to high. Sear the meat well on all sides, then remove to a plate.

Add the onions and brown sugar to the pot and reduce the heat to medium-low. Cook, stirring occasionally, for about 20 minutes, or until the onions are soft and caramelized to a deep golden brown. Stir in the garlic and cook for 2 more minutes.

Raise the heat to medium-high. Pour in the beer and scrape the bottom of the pot with a wooden spoon to dislodge any brown bits. Bring to a boil, then add the reserved bacon and the meat along with any accumulated juices. Add the chicken stock (you may need more than a cup to cover the meat), bay leaf, and thyme, and bring to a low simmer. Reduce the heat, cover, and simmer until the meat is very tender, about 2 hours.

Before serving, uncover and raise the heat to medium to bring the stew to a fast simmer. Simmer for about 10 minutes, or until the liquids are reduced to a sauce-like consistency. Stir in the vinegar or lemon juice and check the seasoning, adding salt and pepper as needed. Serve the stew over buttered egg noodles, if desired, topping each bowl with a sprinkling of parsley.

▶ **DRINK PAIRING** Break out the good beers to accompany this meal: Gulden Draak from Belgium, for instance, or for a domestic choice, the Raison d'Être from Delaware's Dogfish Head Brewery.

HOW TO SERVE THE GATEWAY DUCK

As much as we all love to cook and eat wild game, one of the most rewarding things to do with this food is share it with others—especially those who don't get to enjoy it as often as we do. When you're cooking for non-hunters or wild-game beginners, it's important not to go too wild. As delicious as braised venison tongue (page 61) is, that's the meal to save for more experienced and adventurous diners. The goal here is to keep your guests coming back for seconds, and to do that you need to cook with ingredients that are simple, familiar, and delicious.

This recipe—which calls for that most universally simple, familiar, and delicious ingredient, bacon—is all but guaranteed to change even the pickiest eater's mind about wild ducks. I've heard people call these duck bites, bits, or even rumquackie, but I like to call them the Gateway Duck—because one taste leads to the hard stuff: roast duck, seared breast, even confit.

Start by chunking a skinned duck breast into walnut-size pieces. Pour a bottle of cheap Italian dressing over the top and marinate overnight. Get a piece of pickled jalapeño or, if you can't handle the kick, a water chestnut and wrap it and a hunk of duck with a whole slice of bacon. Secure with a toothpick. Drop onto a hot grill and roll them around as the fat sizzles away. Grill just until the bacon crisps, but not so long the duck is anywhere past medium. Before you pull them off the heat, drizzle honey over the top.

And while I know I said it's important to share, there's no shame in sneaking a few of these for yourself before serving. —D.D.

BACKCOUNTRY PAELLA

Chef Jeff Blank of Austin, Texas devised this recipe after being challenged to a paella cook-off during a weekend hunt in the Texas Hill Country. Paella is the Spanish ancestor of jambalaya—meats and seafood simmered with rice. Blank's cooking philosophy is about "turning your kitchen into a trip around the world, a safari, an Alaskan fishing adventure." This dish is laden with rabbit, duck, and venison, and takes good old American game on a Spanish odyssey.

SERVES 6

1 lb (500 g) venison backstrap

1 wild duck

8 oz (250 g) rabbit

Salt and freshly ground black pepper to taste

4½ cups (36 fl oz/1.1 l) chicken stock

½ cup (4 fl oz/125 ml) dry white wine

1 teaspoon saffron

¾ cup (6 fl oz/180 ml) plus 2 tablespoons olive oil

½ cup (2½ oz/75 g) diced red and green bell peppers

2 cups (6 oz/185 g) chopped green onions

10 cloves garlic, minced

1½ cups (6 oz/185 g) frozen or jarred pearl onions

1 can (14 oz/440 g) crushed tomatoes

½ cup (3½ oz/105 g) cooked (or frozen) lima beans

2 cups (8 oz/250 g) frozen quartered artichoke hearts

½ cup (2½ oz/75 g) peas

3 teaspoons sweet paprika

4 sprigs rosemary

3 cups (21 oz/655 g) medium-grain rice such as Arborio

Season the meats with salt and pepper and grill to medium-rare. (Or, like Blank, cook them in a smoker to the same doneness.) When the meats are cool enough to handle, cut them (deboning as necessary) into ½-inch (12-mm) pieces and set aside.

Bring the stock, wine, and saffron to a low simmer in a medium saucepan. Heat the olive oil in a paella pan or a large, deep cast-iron skillet over high heat until almost smoking, then add the peppers, green onions, garlic, and pearl onions. Cook until softened, about 5 minutes.

Reduce the heat to medium-high and add the tomatoes, lima beans, artichoke hearts, peas, paprika, and rosemary. Cook for another 2 minutes.

Stir the rice into the pan until it's well coated with the oil. Add the warm stock mixture to the pan, and simmer, stirring often, until it's no longer soupy but still very moist.

Add the meats to the pan and remove it from the heat. Cover with a lid or tightly with aluminum foil. Let sit for another 10–15 minutes to allow the rice to fully absorb the liquids. Taste and season with salt and pepper, and serve.

THE ICE FISHERMAN'S BREAKFAST

Here's the perfect starter to a long, languorous day in an ice shanty. Though we tend to reach for the bacon or sausage, fish and eggs are a classic breakfast combination in many places around the world—and for good reason, because they're great together. Even greater, of course, when the fish was just moments ago dancing on the end of a jigging rod.

SERVES 2

1 cup (8 fl oz/250 ml) buttermilk
1½ cups all-purpose flour
½ cup (3½ oz/105 g) cornmeal
Salt and freshly ground pepper
2 tablespoons vegetable oil
2 tablespoons butter, or as needed
4 perch fillets
4 eggs

Pour the buttermilk into a shallow bowl, and in another bowl or plate, combine the flour and cornmeal with generous dashes of salt and pepper.

In a cast-iron skillet, heat the oil and the butter over medium heat. While the oil is heating, dip the fillets one by one into the buttermilk, then dredge them in the flour mixture, shaking off any excess. When the oil is hot, lay the fillets in the pan and cook until browned, about 3 minutes per side. Remove the fillets to a plate, and cover loosely with foil.

Reduce the heat to its lowest setting and, if needed, add an additional pat of butter to the pan. Crack the eggs into the pan and cook, slowly and without disturbing them, until the whites are completely set and the yolks have just started to thicken. Sprinkle with salt and pepper to taste, and serve beside the fillets.

▶ **DRINK PAIRING** Life is different inside an ice shanty. Beer, for instance, is a perfectly acceptable breakfast drink. I'm fond of a bizarrely tasty morning variation of the classic Shandy (beer plus lemonade) in which orange juice replaces the lemonade. Though sometimes called a Brass Monkey or a Beermosa, I call it a Shanty. A fisherman needs his vitamin C, after all.

SPRING

Spring is a season of water: the snowmelt that comes pouring down slopes, the relentless rains that turn the ground to squish, the thawing streams stretching themselves awake as the days grow slowly longer. And because it's a season of water, it's a season of angling. Come April, the trout fishermen enact their own version of a hatch, thronging streamsides to tickle the water's surface with an Adams or a Royal Wulff fly. When the first dogwood blossoms appear, bass anglers know that the spawn has begun, though many bassers will have already been fishing the pre-spawn, reeling their lures slowly through the water to attract these groggy, early-season bass. And then there's the spring walleye, lurking close to the fresh greenery of newly-emerging weeds. The fish are hungry after their long, metabolic slumber, and the anglers are, too—no fish tastes better than those pulled from cold water, and none can match that ineffable first-of-the-season flavor.

Despite all this flocking to water, however, the woods are far from barren. Spring turkey hunters are sitting stone-still against tree trunks, calling in gobblers, while in other places the spring bear hunt goes into full swing. This is also a prime time for foraging: For an inland interpretation of surf-'n'-turf, those fiddlehead ferns unspooling from the soft streamside soil are the perfect companion to a freshly-grilled trout. Look for the wild asparagus, as well, concealing itself among riverside briars. Many flavors are at their peak in spring, requiring the cook to do very little save to let them shine—just as the sun is finally shining, too.

TROUT WITH FIDDLEHEADS & SCRAMBLED EGGS

Right about the time trout anglers start appearing on streamsides, something else pops up in wild clumps along the waterways—fiddlehead ferns, which have a nutty, asparagus-like flavor that is prized by foragers and chefs alike. If you can't find them, substitute inch-long segments of asparagus.

SERVES 2

2 slices bacon

Salt and freshly ground black pepper

1 or 2 trout, depending on size, cleaned

3 tablespoons butter

1 big handful fiddlehead ferns (about 1 cup/3 oz/90 g), trimmed and rinsed

Juice of 1 lemon

4 eggs

2 tablespoons milk, lemon juice, or water

2 thick slices country bread, toasted

Preheat the oven to 400°F (200°C). In a large, ovenproof skillet, cook the bacon over medium-high heat until barely crisp, and remove to drain, leaving the bacon grease in the skillet. When cooled, crumble the bacon. Meanwhile, generously salt and pepper the trout inside and out. Add 1 tablespoon of the butter to the skillet along with the trout and cook, without disturbing, until the skin is golden and crisping, about 3 minutes. Flip the trout, and transfer the skillet to the oven to cook for an additional couple of minutes.

In another skillet over medium-high heat, melt another 1 tablespoon of the butter and add the fiddlehead ferns. Cook, covered, 3–4 minutes. Uncover, add the lemon juice, and continue to cook, another 3 minutes, stirring to deglaze the pan. The fiddleheads are done when they're tender but faintly crunchy, like asparagus.

While the fiddleheads are cooking, whisk the eggs and milk in a bowl and season with salt and pepper. Add the remaining 1 tablespoon butter, the egg mixture, and the crumbled bacon to the fiddleheads, then reduce the heat to medium-low. Cook 3–4 minutes, stirring gently, until the eggs are curdled and creamy but still a bit runny.

Serve the eggs alongside the trout, with a thick slice of toasted bread.

HOW TO FORAGE FOR FIDDLEHEADS

As hunters, we're tapping into only half of our primitive potential. When we're bent to the track, our hearts pound, bringing us closer to the way our ancestors lived. Meanwhile, we relegate the gatherer in our bloodstream to the supermarket. Change that this spring by foraging for fiddleheads.

Named for the way their leaves curl, fiddleheads are the young shoots of the ostrich fern. Pick the coiled, gray-green fronds when they are about an inch (2.5 cm) in diameter and an inch tall (the taller they are, the older and less desirable). Best harvested in early spring, the recommended picking strategy is 3 tops per plant. Each plant produces 7 that turn into fronds; over-picking will kill the plant (not to mention your karma for responsible, sustainable foraging).

Native to the Northeast and upper Midwestern states in the U.S., these plants are covered with brown papery scales that sometimes partially peel away. Though they're sometimes available regionally in certain supermarkets or restaurants, they're not cultivated and remain purely seasonal—a welcome change from the import/export vegetable trade.

Keep in mind that undercooked fiddleheads can cause headaches and upset stomach. So make sure they're tender before eating. —K.M.

FREEZER-RAID GUMBO

Gumbo is an example of Cajun cookery's prime directive—waste not, want not. This makes it the perfect dish for using up any odds and ends in the deep-freeze.

SERVES 12

STOCK

1 large wild duck, or 2 small ones, cleaned and quartered

About 3 lb (1.5 kg) mixed wild game (quail, dove, goose, squirrel, rabbit, raccoon, venison, etc., dressed and cut into manageable pieces)

1 yellow onion, quartered

4 ribs celery, roughly chopped

4 carrots, roughly chopped

½ cup (4 fl oz/125 ml) vegetable oil

Salt and freshly ground pepper

¾ cup (6 fl oz/180 ml) vegetable oil

½ cup (2½ oz/75 g) all-purpose flour

1 yellow onion, chopped

1 cup (5 oz/155 g) chopped green bell pepper

½ cup (2½ oz/75 g) chopped celery

¼ cup (¾ oz/20 g) chopped green onions

3 cloves garlic, minced

1 lb (500 g) andouille or other smoked sausage, sliced into ½-inch (12-mm) pieces

1 bay leaf

½ teaspoon dried thyme

2 cups (10 oz/315 g) sliced okra

¼ cup (⅓ oz/10 g) chopped fresh Italian parsley

Steamed white rice for serving

MAKE THE STOCK Preheat the oven to 400°F (200°C). In a large roasting pan, combine the duck and game with the onion, celery, and carrots. Drizzle with vegetable oil and toss to coat. Salt and pepper generously, then place in the oven for 30 minutes. Transfer the contents to a 2-gallon (8-l) stockpot and add cold water to cover. Bring to a boil, then lower the heat and simmer, uncovered, for 1½ hours. Remove and reserve the meat, picking out bones and fat. Strain the stock, discard the vegetables and other solids, and return about 3 qt (3 l) of the strained liquid to the stockpot. Keep it simmering as you start the next step.

Combine ½ cup (4 fl oz/125 ml) of the oil and the flour in a wide, heavy skillet over medium-high heat, whisking constantly. As the mixture browns, keep whisking (to prevent the flour from burning) until it resembles chocolate syrup (3–4 minutes). Immediately add the chopped onion, bell pepper, celery, green onions, garlic, and sausage. Cook, stirring, until the vegetables are wilted. Transfer the mixture to the stock and stir until evenly blended. Add the reserved meat, bay leaf, and thyme.

Wipe out the skillet. Heat the remaining ¼ cup oil until it shimmers. Cook the okra, stirring, until it is no longer ropy and slimy. Add the okra to the stockpot and simmer, covered, for about 1½ hours. Add the parsley and salt and pepper to taste, and serve over rice.

BLACK BEAR EMPANADAS

John Reilly, a New York City catering chef and hunter, wowed guests at a *Field & Stream* dinner with these hot pockets filled with currants, cilantro, and the meat of a black bear from one of his hunting trips to Manitoba, Canada. Reilly is a big fan of bear meat, which suffers a poor reputation for being greasy—but improper field dressing is mostly to blame. "You've got to remove all the fat," he advises. "It's a dark meat, a little on the sweet side, with a rich, rich flavor." If you're an unlucky bear hunter, venison would be a fine stand-in for bear meat.

DRY RUB

1 cup (7 oz/220 g) dark brown sugar

¼ cup (2 oz/60 g) kosher salt

1 tablespoon black pepper

2 tablespoons ground dried chipotle or poblano chile, or chili powder

¼ cup (1 oz/30 g) onion powder

2 tablespoons garlic powder

1 tablespoon ground cumin

1 tablespoon cinnamon

Zest of 4 oranges, finely grated

EMPANADAS

One 8- to 10-lb (4- to 5-kg) bear leg, haunch, or ham (butt portion of the leg), boned, all fat trimmed

½ cup (4 fl oz/125 ml) olive oil

2–3 Spanish or red onions, roughly chopped

3 carrots, peeled and roughly chopped

3 ribs celery, roughly chopped

6–8 cloves garlic, roughly chopped

1 can (6 oz/185 g) tomato paste

12 fl oz (375 ml) stout beer

4–5 qt (4–5 l) beef stock

2 cups (12 oz/375 g) dried currants

1 bunch cilantro, leaves picked

2–3 packages Goya empanada wrappers

2 eggs

MAKE THE DRY RUB Combine all the rub ingredients and mix well.

Generously coat the bear leg with the dry rub. Allow to sit for at least 3–4 hours, or up to overnight, in the refrigerator.

Preheat the oven to 325°F (165°C). Heat the olive oil in a large pot or Dutch oven over medium heat. Brown the bear leg on all sides, taking care not to let the sugar burn. Remove the meat from the pot and set aside.

Add the onions, carrots, celery, and garlic to the pot and sauté until the onions are softening and beginning to brown, 7–10 minutes. Stir in the tomato paste. Return the bear meat to the pot and add the stout and enough stock to almost cover the meat. Bring the liquid to a boil.

Cover the pot and put it in the oven. Cook until the meat is soft and fork-tender, stirring occasionally and adding more stock as needed, 4–6 hours. Remove the meat from the liquid and let it rest until it cools to room temperature. Reserve the cooked vegetables and 2 cups (16 fl oz/500 ml) of the liquid and let cool completely. Once cooled, place these in a food processor or blender and process until smooth. Set aside.

To make the filling, pull the meat apart into shreds, discarding any sinew, then chop into small pieces. In a large mixing bowl, combine the chopped meat with the currants and cilantro, and add just enough of the reserved cooking liquid to moisten and bind the meat. It should not be wet.

To make the empanadas, following the package directions for the empanada wrappers, fill each empanada with about 2 oz (60 g) of filling. Brush the outside of the empanadas with an egg wash made from whisking the 2 eggs with 2 tablespoons water. Chill thoroughly (they can also be frozen at this point) on a parchment-lined sheet pan.

When you are ready to bake the empanadas, preheat the oven to 350°F (180°C). Arrange the empanadas 2 inches (5 cm) apart on a sheet pan lined with fresh parchment paper and bake until golden brown, 15–25 minutes. (Frozen empanadas should be thawed before baking.) Serve hot.

LITTLE FISH, BIG FLAVOR

Panfishing, for adults, is primarily a culinary act. The very fact that we gather sunfish, crappie, and several perch species under the collective banner of "panfish"—by which we mean, fish sized to fit squarely inside a frying pan—attests to this. While some degree of boyish sport is involved in landing a palm-sized bluegill, the landing is usually mere foreplay to eating that bluegill, ideally after it's been fried whole and served atop some newspaper beside green onions and a lemon wedge. I am old enough now and intermittently confident in my abilities to find and catch the sorts of big-muscled fish that make women swoon and children clap, to confess the following: On most days, I'd rather bust into a school of crappie or bream than, say, release a trophy steelhead. The pleasures of panfishing—the scrappy fights, the fast and steady action, the fish on the stringer small and shiny like new coins, and of course the cooking and eating—seem to sink a little deeper, down past the ego to the soul, which I've always thought lies somewhere close beside the belly. Sport and skill and experience and devotion are intricately involved in the pursuit of larger, more glamorous fish; panfishing, on the other hand, entails mostly pure joy, and then some napkins.

The vast majority of panfish in this country arrive at the table fried, and there's a good reason for that—few fish fry up better than bluegills, crappie, and perch. An acquaintance of mine once lived happily on nothing but fried bluegills—this was in Mississippi, where we call them bream—for thirty straight days and nights, eating six or eight daily and, local legend has it, never changing the grease. By any stretch this is gratuitous behavior, but I can't think of any other fried fish—save catfish, maybe—that the stomach and brain would exclusively accept for such a prolonged interlude. Though subtle, even whispery flavor differences exist between the panfish species, all boast firm, flaky-white meat and a mild, clean, even creamy taste (in Louisiana, that creaminess lends crappie its local name, *sac au lait*, which is French for "bag of milk"). I've always tended to fry panfish whole—cleaned, scaled, with just the head removed—for two reasons: One, filleting a mess of panfish is a chore worth avoiding, and two (with young bluegills, especially) the crispy fried tails are outlandishly delicious. Think piscatorial pork rinds.

Yet panfish eat equally well without vats of grease getting involved. With their solid flakes and unobtrusive flavor, cubed panfish fillets are a natural base for camp chowders. Simply sauté diced onions, celery, carrots, and potatoes in bacon grease, add water or fish stock to cover, then simmer for a half hour or so; add some sliced panfish fillets, diced bacon, and as much half-and-half as your heart will allow, simmer for another five minutes, and then find a chair and a big spoon. The flaky meat is also a natural choice for fish cakes, which make grand fish-camp breakfasts as well as a champion starter course for dinner, dressed up with a good sauce. Fish cakes are also a savvy use for those leftover bream from last night's fish fry, and the cakes can be mashed together with pretty much any ingredients you have at hand. Panfish are indulgent that way—they're easy enough to catch, usually in bounteous numbers, that cooking them should be a stress-free operation. Take all the breezy risks you want; if you screw up a batch, simply catch some more.

For most of us, the first fish we ever caught and ate was a panfish—in most cases, a fish guided out of the water and into a pan by a father or grandfather. If you're like me, the first bite of that small fish was a momentous one, a hot forkful of flavor sauced with a dazzling, renewed understanding of the natural order of life. Many of us, in our march toward bigger fish and brawnier challenges, tend to forget how delicious and important those early panfish were, or imagine that our memories of those forkfuls have been sugared with nostalgia. Not so: Those first panfish tasted that good because they were that good. And they still are.

ULTIMATE FRIED BREAM (TAILS & ALL)

This recipe comes via Hershel Ladner, who hosts a fish fry at his hunting camp near Wiggins, Mississippi, every summer for his fellow directors of the Mississippi Deep Sea Fishing Rodeo, and who has been catching and cooking bream for close to seven decades. Scoring the bream along their backbones makes eating the bream a blessedly boneless task—the meat slides right off the ribs. Very small bluegills can be eaten whole, bones and all. And be sure to eat the crunchy-fried tails, which some folks (me included) consider the best part.

SERVES 4

8 bluegills (bream), gutted and scaled with heads removed

2 cups (10 oz/315 g) yellow corn flour*

Salt and freshly ground pepper

¼ cup (2 fl oz/60 ml) peanut or vegetable oil

*Corn flour is extra-finely ground cornmeal. Cornmeal works, too—the difference is purely textural. (Try combining them for a slighty gritty, slightly fine crust.) Do not, however, confuse cornstarch for corn flour.

With a sharp knife, score the bluegills along both sides of their backbones. Don't cut too deep (just about ¼ inch/6 mm)—you're just looking to let some oil in there to loosen up the meat.

Heat an iron skillet or other heavy pan over medium-high heat.

Place the corn flour on a plate or shallow pan and season with salt and pepper. Lightly dredge a fish in the corn flour, shaking off any excess. Add the oil to the pan; when it's hot and shimmery, add the fish. Jiggle the pan for the first 5 or 10 seconds to keep the fish from sticking. Cook until a golden crust forms on the fish, then carefully turn it over and cook the other side until golden brown. Drain on paper towels, then remove to a warm plate or a cookie sheet placed in a 200°F (95°C) oven. Repeat with the rest of the fish, adding more oil as necessary. Serve with lemon wedges, green onions, white bread, or whatever else you please.

HOW TO RAISE A FISHING BUDDY

Rigging live bait is a building block that can serve as the baby steps in an outdoor relationship with your child that can lead you, literally, to the ends of the earth. Take it lightheartedly, but not lightly.

USE THE RIGHT HOOK Small hands demand an Aberdeen hook. This style has a long shank that is easy to grasp and a relatively wide cap that makes it easy to slip out of a fish's mouth. Be sure to use the smallest sizes you can get away with. You need action to keep your child hooked, and a bucket of runt bream count for more than one bragging-size fish.

GIVE FISH THE SLIP The harder a fish has to work to pull a float under, the less likely it is to keep the hook. Smaller or weighted bobbers create less buoyancy and lessen the resistance a fish feels. To make for much easier casting, use a slip-bobber rig with a knot and bead. It's no fun trying to cast a bobber and 6 feet of trailing line.

DOUBLE UP Stretch a nightcrawler between two small hooks tied in tandem. This presents a natural-looking bait in the water and helps catch short-striking fish.

EAT YOUR CATCH Now and then, try to keep a few fish for the dinner table. After all, you and your child just dipped your hands in waters that have sustained human life for eons. It's an important lesson, and something to celebrate with a grander gesture than a candy bar on the drive home. —T.E.N.

OAT-CRUSTED TROUT WITH STOVIES

If you're trout fishing in the lochs of Scotland, this is how your catch should end up—batter-crusted with that ubiquitous Scottish staple, oats, and served beside a generous mound of stovies (Scottish slang for stove-roasted potatoes). Round it off with a pint of stout to complete your British Isles fish fry.

SERVES 4

STOVIES

¼ cup (2 fl oz/60 ml) vegetable oil

2 large yellow onions, thinly sliced

1½ lb (750 g) new potatoes, thinly sliced

Salt and freshly ground black pepper

½ cup (4 fl oz/125 ml) beef stock

2 tablespoons fresh chives, minced

TROUT

1 egg

½ cup (4 fl oz/125 ml) milk

All-purpose flour for dredging

4 whole trout, cleaned

1 cup (3 oz/90 g) rolled oats

2 tablespoons vegetable oil, or as needed

MAKE THE STOVIES In a large pot or Dutch oven, heat the vegetable oil over medium-high heat until almost smoking. Add the onions and potatoes, and stir well to coat evenly. Generously season with salt and pepper. Cover the pot and reduce the heat to medium-low. After 10 minutes, add the beef stock, stir, and replace the lid. Cook until the potatoes are just tender, about 20 minutes more. Increase the heat to medium-high, and cook, uncovered, for 5 minutes to brown the potatoes. Sprinkle with chives and keep warm.

MAKE THE TROUT In a medium bowl, whisk the egg and milk together. In a separate dish, mix flour with generous dashes of salt and pepper. Rinse the trout with cold water and pat dry with paper towels. Lightly dredge the fish in the seasoned flour, then in the egg mixture (or use a pastry brush to coat the fish). Roll the fish in the oats, pressing lightly to make sure they adhere.

Heat 2 tablespoons oil in a large skillet over medium-high heat. Add the trout in batches (you may need to add more oil as you go), and cook until golden brown, 3–4 minutes per side. Flip them as gently as possible. Transfer the fish to a low (200°F/95°C) oven as they're finished, then serve promptly beside a mound of stovies.

▶ **DRINK PAIRING** For obvious reasons, an oatmeal stout—like the one brewed by Samuel Smith—goes well with this dish. Oatmeal stouts were popular in the late nineteenth century but had all but disappeared by World War I; Samuel Smith revived them in 1980. Better yet, accompany this with a wee dram of single-malt Scotch. Glenfiddich's 15-year-old Solera Reserve, matured in sherry, bourbon, and new oak barrels, pairs smoothly with the trout.

PREPPING YOUR CATCH

So, you've caught your limit. Before it's time to heat the peanut oil, you'll need to hone your fillet knife. Let's assume you've mastered the basics; what follows are a few advanced cleaning techniques—plus an easy trick to kill freezer burn with the fish you save for later.

BUTTERFLY A TROUT

Trout and salmon are much thicker near the head than at the tail, and cooking larger ones whole on a grill tends to produce an uneven result. To more consistently cook these fish, butterfly them first. It's a bit like the old Italian technique of grilling a butterflied chicken under a brick—makes the cooking quicker and more even.

1 Start by removing the head, slitting the belly, and removing the entrails, as usual. Then, with the fish on its side, make a small cut immediately ahead of the tail down to the backbone on one side.

2 Turn the fish on its back and make a downward cut inside the body cavity along the entire length next to the backbone. This cut should be on the same side of the backbone as the previous tail cut. Slice through the ribs and down to, but not through, the skin of the back.

3 The dorsal skin will act as a hinge as you fold the cut half outward and flat. Once cooked, the ribs and backbone will easily lift free. —J. Merwin

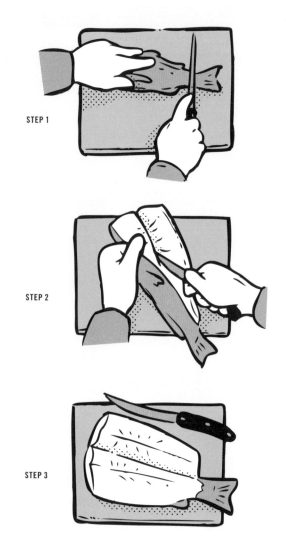

STEP 1

STEP 2

STEP 3

SKIN A CATFISH

Back in your grandpa's day, skinning a catfish meant nailing the sucker to a backyard pine tree and stripping the skin with pliers. It doesn't take much to bring the old-timer's technique into the twenty-first century for the same results. Here's how:

SCORE IT Place a 3-foot (1-meter)-long 2x6 board on a level, waist-high surface. (A truck tailgate works well.) Using a knife, score the skin all the way around the head, just in front of the cat's gill plates. Make another slit down the fish's back.

PEEL IT Drive a 16-penny nail through the fish's skull to secure it to the board. Cut off its dorsal fin. Brace the board against your waist, with the tail pointing toward you. Grasp the skin with some pliers and pull it down to the tail and off.

GUT IT Remove the fish from the board. Grasping the head in one hand and the body in the other, bend the head sharply downward, breaking the spine. Now bend the body up and twist to separate head from body. Open the belly with your knife, remove the remaining viscera from the body cavity, and rinse well. These instructions are for eating-size cats—say, 4 lb (1.8 kg) or less. Anything larger, and you'll have to whack the head off with a cleaver. —T.E.N.

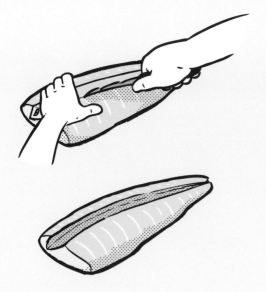

FILLET A NORTHERN PIKE

The Y-bones embedded in the dorsal flesh of a northern pike prevent many anglers from dining on one of the tastiest fish that swims. Learn to remove them and you will never again curse when a 3-pound pike bashes your walleye rig.

1 Fillet the fish, removing flesh from the ribs as you would with any other fish.

2 Find the row of white dots visible midway between the spine and the top of the fillet. These are the tips of the Y-bones. Slice along the top of these dots, nearly through the fillet, following the curvature of the bones.

3 Slice along the bottom of the Y-bones, following their shape, aiming the knife tip toward the first incision.

4 Connect the two cuts above the fish's anus. Remove the bony strip. Get the grease popping. —T.E.N.

FREEZE YOUR CATCH

The enemy of successful, long-term freezing is air. When air meets food, dehydration occurs, leading to freezer burn. With delicate proteins like fish, freezer burn can be downright fatal, ruining both texture and flavor. If you don't own a vacuum sealer, freeze your catch in a block of ice. This locks out any corrupting air by sealing the fish in a familiar element—water. This is best done with fillets, though whole cleaned fish can be frozen this way too.

1 Scale and gut the fish. If fillets are what you'll be cooking, fillet all fish instead, and portion the fillets so that you won't be thawing more than you'll be eating.

2 Put the fish in a large container and fill with water. Knock the sides to roust any air bubbles. Place in the freezer until the water is solid.

3 Transfer the ice to a freezer bag. Label the bag, and return to the freezer. To defrost, place the block in a bowl and allow it to melt in the refrigerator.

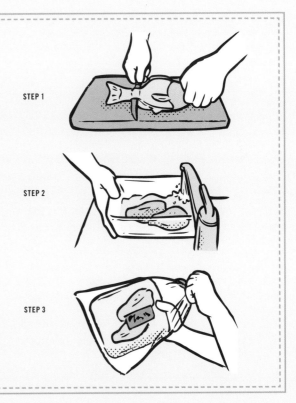

STEP 1

STEP 2

STEP 3

PICKLED PIKE

Pickled pike is a classic North Country treat, but it also boasts a practical aspect: The acid in the vinegar dissolves the dreaded Y-bones that make filleting pike such a chore. (For boneless trout or walleye fillets, you can skip the soaking step.) Pickled pike is fantastic served on toasted rye bread, with a dab of butter, but it's equally good on a Ritz cracker accompanied by an ice-cold can of Old Milwaukee (or your favorite choice). One thing to note: Due to tapeworm concerns, use pike that's been frozen for at least 48 hours, which kills those parasites.

SERVES 6

1 cup (8 oz/250 g) kosher salt

1 lb (500 g) northern pike fillets, cut into 1-inch (2.5-cm) chunks

1 qt (32 fl oz/1 l) distilled white vinegar

¾ cup (8 oz/185 g) sugar

1-inch (2.5-cm) piece fresh horseradish, peeled and thinly sliced

4 slices fresh ginger, about the size of a quarter

4 whole cloves

2 teaspoons whole allspice berries

2 teaspoons whole yellow mustard seeds

½ teaspoon whole black peppercorns

¼ teaspoon cayenne pepper (optional)

3 bay leaves

2 cloves garlic, peeled

1 carrot, peeled and thinly sliced

1 red onion, thinly sliced

Make a brine by combining the salt with 1 qt (32 fl oz/1 l) water in a nonreactive bowl or pan. Add the pieces of pike to the brine and soak for 24 hours. Discard the brine, replacing it with the vinegar, and soak for an additional 24 hours. Remove the fish, reserving 1 cup (8 fl oz/250 ml) of the vinegar for use in the pickling solution, and then refrigerate.

Combine the reserved cup of vinegar with ½ cup (4 fl oz/125 ml) water and the sugar in a nonaluminum saucepan over high heat. Bring to a boil, stirring to dissolve, then remove from the heat and let cool.

In a 1-quart mason jar, add a quarter of the fish, then add some of the spices, a clove of garlic, and then sliced carrot and onion; repeat with the remainder of the fish, spices, and vegetables so that the ingredients are evenly layered. Pour the vinegar mixture into the jar. Cover tightly and refrigerate for at least 3 days to allow the flavors to develop.

▶ **SERVING TIP** Top your favorite cracker with a dollop and enjoy. Leftovers will keep, refrigerated, for up to a month.

HOW TO MAKE SMOKED SALMON DIP

So long as you're pickling fish, why not pair it with preserved fish? Smoked salmon, for example. For any party, this dip is easy to make and always impresses. You'll want to whip up a big batch, because it won't last long.

If you don't have some smoked salmon lying around, try befriending a salmon fisherman. As a last resort, you can pick up a package at most grocery stores, but do me a favor: Catch your own salmon by this time next year.

- Once you've procured your smoked salmon, shred it in a bowl using two forks. You could use a food processor, but then you'd have to clean it.

- Dice some green onions and add them to the salmon, along with some capers if you're into that sort of thing.

- Next, put a big scoop of sour cream in the bowl, followed by a squirt of lemon juice.

- Mix all this together, adding more sour cream until you get the consistency you prefer—chunky or creamy.

- If you're feeling a bit frisky, sprinkle in a pinch or two of spicy red pepper flakes.

A great smoked salmon dip is as simple as that, and it's infinitely variable. Don't be afraid to experiment with Tabasco, Worcestershire, mustard, celery (seed or diced), or anything else. And the best thing to spread it on? Saltine crackers. It's that simple.
—D.D.

I have commitment issues. I don't have one favorite pocketknife; I have seven. One week, my go-to drink is a Manhattan, the next it's an Old Fashioned, then I'm on a Sazerac kick. (At least I can settle on bourbon—though sometimes I prefer rye.) And if you were to open my fridge, you'd find a dozen different bottles of hot sauce.

It's impossible for me to pick a favorite, but when it comes to fish and wild game, there's one bottle of fire I reach for more than any other: Sriracha. If you've never tried Sriracha, turn down the hot-sauce aisle during your next trip to the grocery store and look for the bottle with the white rooster and the green cap.

Thick, garlicky, and (seriously) hot, Sriracha cranks up the flavor on just about everything. I love it drizzled over hash, fish tacos, or a venison steak sandwich, but Sriracha shines brightest with Asian flavors—no surprise, given its Thai roots. It's the perfect finishing touch to a stir-fry and gives our wild-game *báhn mì* (at right) just enough sinus-clearing heat.

Just keep in mind that a little bit goes a long way. With Sriracha, the last thing you want to do is overcommit. —C.K.

WILD-GAME BÁNH MÌ

Bánh mì (pronounced BUN-mee) is a seriously addictive type of Vietnamese sandwich. The zesty flavors make it a natural vehicle for any wild game—here, meat from game that gets worked into patties. East meets West? More like East meets Wild.

MAKES 12 PATTIES

½ cup (4 fl oz/125 ml) mayonnaise

3–5 tablespoons Sriracha (*at left*) or other hot sauce

2 lb (1 kg) wild game, such as venison or boar; or gamebirds like pheasant, duck, or wild turkey, boned and roughly chopped (optional: skin included)

2–3 habanero chiles, seeded if desired (for extra heat, leave seeds in)

1 teaspoon coriander seed

⅓ cup (3 fl oz/80 ml) Vietnamese or Thai fish sauce

1 tablespoon sugar

½ teaspoon cinnamon

2 teaspoons baking powder

Baguette, split and lightly toasted

1 cup (½ oz/15 g) cilantro leaves

Combine the mayonnaise and Sriracha sauce, and refrigerate until ready to use.

Preheat the oven to 300°F (150°C). Combine the meat, skin (if using), chiles, coriander, fish sauce, sugar, cinnamon, and baking powder in a bowl. Working in batches, grind the mixture into a paste using a food processor with the blade attachment. You want it finely ground, with no chunks or strands of sinew.

With an ice-cream scoop, spoon the mixture onto a parchment-lined or nonstick sheet pan. Gently flatten each ball into a hamburger-style patty. Bake for 30 minutes, or until the patties are thoroughly cooked and a meat thermometer inserted into the center of a patty reads 160°F (71°C).

Slather the cooled bread with the Sriracha mayonnaise and top with a big pinch of cilantro. Lay on the hot patty, and close it up with the remaining piece of bread to form a sandwich.

ESSENTIAL KNIVES

Truth is, a sharp chef's knife is the only blade you absolutely need in your kitchen. But, since no outdoorsman—or wild chef—could ever be satisfied with just one knife, here are seven.

BOWIE Unsheath this beast once a year—to carve a Fourth of July watermelon.

FILLET Aside from its intended use—carving fish—a sharp, flexible fillet knife is invaluable when butchering big game.

BONING The slender blade and sharp point allow for precise, controlled cuts, which you'll need when deboning a duck or pheasant.

CHEF'S Here's your do-it-all slicer, dicer, chopper, and carver. Invest in the best one you can afford, and keep the edge sharp and straight.

CLEAVER This workhorse is essential for breaking down small game and gamebirds—and it doubles as a meat mallet.

SERRATED Reserve this blade for bread as well as delicate fruits and vegetables.

PARING After the chef's knife, this is your second must-have. It's designed for peeling, coring, and other intricate cuts.

WILD TURKEY POTPIE

Banish all memories of the frozen supermarket potpies you ate in childhood. This pie boasts an ultraflaky crust that caps a luscious mixture of winter squash, herbs, and wild turkey. If using leftover cooked turkey, skip the browning.

CRUST

1½ cups (7½ oz/235 g) all-purpose flour

1–1½ teaspoons freshly ground black pepper

½ teaspoon salt

8 tablespoons (1 stick/4 oz/125 g) chilled unsalted butter, cubed

¼ cup (2 fl oz/60 ml) ice water, or as needed

FILLING

3 tablespoons olive oil

2½ lb (125 kg) boneless, skinless wild turkey meat, cut into 1-inch (2.5-cm) pieces

3 cloves garlic, minced

3 ribs celery, diced

1 cup (5 oz/155 g) butternut squash, diced

1 cup (4 oz/125 g) pearl onions

3 cups (24 fl oz/750 ml) chicken stock

5 tablespoons (2½ oz/75 g) butter

½ cup (2½ oz/75 g) all-purpose flour

1 cup (8 fl oz/250 ml) milk

⅓ cup (3 fl oz/80 ml) light cream

3 tablespoons chopped fresh rosemary

1 egg

2 tablespoons water

MAKE THE CRUST In a food processor, pulse together the flour, pepper, and salt, then scatter in the butter and pulse until the mixture resembles coarse crumbs. Sprinkle in the ice water and pulse again, until the dough starts to come together and pull away from the sides. Transfer it to a floured surface. You should be able to form it into a shaggy ball, but add more cold water—a tablespoon at a time—if it won't come together. Flatten the ball into a thick disk, wrap in plastic wrap, and refrigerate for at least 30 minutes.

MAKE THE FILLING Preheat the oven to 375°F (190°C). In a sauté pan, heat 2 tablespoons of the olive oil over medium-high heat. Generously season the turkey with salt and pepper. Add it to the pan and cook, stirring once in a while, until browned. Remove the turkey with a slotted spoon and set aside. Add the remaining tablespoon of oil to the pan along with the garlic, celery, and squash, and cook until the vegetables soften. Set aside.

Meanwhile, cook the pearl onions: Bring a medium saucepan of water to boil. Trim off the root ends of the onions and boil them for about 10 minutes, then drain and let cool in cold water. When cool enough to handle, peel and trim.

Bring the stock to a boil in a small pot. In a saucepan over medium heat, melt the butter. Whisk in the flour and cook, stirring, for 1 minute. Add the hot stock, the milk, and the cream. Once this mixture boils, turn the heat down to low and let simmer—whisking all the while—until thickened, about 5 minutes. Add the rosemary and season with salt and pepper.

ASSEMBLE THE PIE Add the turkey and vegetables to a large pie dish or other baking dish, followed by the cream mixture. Stir gently to combine.

Roll out the dough on a lightly floured surface to form a circle (or oval, depending on your dish) about an inch wider than the diameter of the dish. Drape it over the dish and pinch the edge into a sealed rim. Use a sharp knife to pop vents in the top.

Make an egg wash by whisking the egg with the water. Brush the dough with this mixture, then bake the pie until the crust is golden and the contents bubbling, about 40 minutes. Serve hot or at room temperature.

DEER DOGS WITH PEA SOUP SAUCE

Pea soup might not be the most popular thing to feed the guys at hunting camp—unless it's served as it is here, slathered on top of fresh venison sausages along with ricotta, mustard, and melted cheese curds. Montreal chef Martin Picard chose to share this recipe because it's the kind of simple food he likes to eat after a hunt. He's welcome at our camp anytime.

SERVES 4

8 venison sausages

Beer, as needed

SAUCE

2 tablespoons olive oil

4 cups (16 oz/500 g) diced yellow onions

4 cups (20 oz/625 g) diced carrots

2 cups (10 oz/315 g) diced celery

4 cups (28 oz/875 g) split peas, soaked for at least 4 hours, or overnight, and drained

8 oz (250 g) smoked pork lard

About 11 oz (345 g) ham, diced

Ricotta cheese for serving

Mustard for serving

8 hot dog buns, toasted

*Tortillons** or other curd cheese for serving

Tortillons are cheese curds you can only get in French-speaking Canada. Feel free to use a local variety.

Soak the sausages in beer for 1 hour. Crack a cold one open for yourself while you're at it.

MAKE THE SAUCE Heat the olive oil in a large pot or Dutch oven over high heat. Sweat the onions, carrots, and celery until the onion becomes translucent (but don't let them brown). Add the peas, pork lard, and 3 qt (3 l) water. Bring to a boil, then lower the heat. Simmer, covered, for 45 minutes. Remove the lard, dice it, and return to the soup. Add the ham. Reduce the heat to low and continue cooking until the soup thickens. Add a dash of olive oil to the reduced pea soup. Stir well.

Meanwhile, cook the dogs in a frying pan. When they're done, set them aside and add ricotta to the residual sausage fat in the pan. Warm the pan over low heat, if necessary, and stir.

Spread mustard and the warmed ricotta mixture on the toasted buns. Add the sausage and a generous spoonful of the pea soup. Dress each dog with cheese curds and brown slightly with a torch. —C.K.

Nearly every part of the deer can be made into jerky. The best cuts are the eye round and rump roast from the hind legs, but any large roast from the hind leg will do. Why? Big cuts mean larger pieces of jerky, and these roasts have most of their muscle fibers running in the same direction. In the world of jerky, this is important.

To our mind, the best jerky is pliable yet chewy—and doesn't make you gnaw on dried muscle fibers longer than your hand. That means cutting against the grain of the meat, in ⅛-inch-thick slices. Don't cut too thin or the venison will dry out like a shingle on your roof. The best way to get this cut every time is to partially freeze the meat: A large roast will need 90 minutes to 2 hours in the chiller before cutting.

Now that we've covered the perfect slice, what about the perfect cooker? There are a number of countertop dehydrators available for cheaper than a commercial model, but most of those have their flaws—mainly a lack of capacity and the need to constantly rotate trays to get an even dry. A commercial dehydrator solves that. An 80-quart model can accommodate up to 10 pounds of meat at a time, and a powerful motor circulates air evenly throughout the interior. Set it, and six hours later you'll have enough jerky to last you the season.

I'll grant you that a commercial dehydrator isn't a small (or cheap) acquisition, and it sucks up a decent chunk of electricity. But that's a small price to pay for the perfect slice of jerky. —D.D. & H.S.

HAWAIIAN FISH JERKY

I first encountered fish jerky during a marlin tournament in Kona, Hawaii. It was steeped in the island flavors of ginger, soy, and pineapple. Here is my best approximation of that Hawaiian treat. Saltwater species like tuna and snapper work great, as do firm-fleshed, low-fat freshwater fish like bass, trout, and crappie.

SERVES 1 BOAT CREW

2 lb (1 kg) firm-fleshed fish fillets

½ cup (4 fl oz/125 ml) soy sauce

¼ cup (2 fl oz/60 ml) pineapple juice

1 tablespoon brown sugar

¼ teaspoon cayenne pepper

1 garlic clove, crushed

1 tablespoon minced fresh ginger

1 teaspoon salt

½ teaspoon freshly ground pepper

Cut the fish into strips ¼ inch (6 mm) thick, 1 inch (2.5 cm) wide, and 3–6 inches (7.5–16 cm) long. Combine the remaining ingredients in a zip-seal bag and marinate the fish in the refrigerator for at least 6 hours, or preferably overnight. Discard the marinade and dry the fish strips well, dabbing them with paper towels to sponge off any excess marinade.

If you own a dehydrator or smoker, use it. Otherwise, you can use a lightly oiled cake rack or oven rack in a low-heated oven. Either way, use the oven's top rack, and be sure to oil the grates to prevent sticking. Put a cookie sheet on the bottom rack to collect any drippings. Place the fish on the rack and set the oven to 145°F (63°C). (Some ovens won't go this low. In that case, set the oven to its minimum temperature and crack the oven door.)

After 2 hours, reduce the heat to 130°F (54°C), or open the door wider. The drying time will vary considerably. When done, the fish jerky will be dry but not brittle, so that the pieces crack but don't break when bent, with a dark brown glaze. Allow the jerky to cool. Keep refrigerated, in a sealed container, until you're ready to eat it.

LARGEMOUTH BASS TACOS

The best largemouth bass fishing I've ever encountered was in Sinaloa, Mexico. We arrived in the midst of a pueblo festival: There were young men playing guitars on corners, local Mayo Indians performing a deer dance, bats fluttering above the trees of the plaza, and street-food vendors everywhere. Here is a recipe for my best imitation of those vendors' fish tacos, which will work with any firm, lean fish.

SERVES 4–6

1 large egg, separated

1 cup (5 oz/155 g) all-purpose flour

Kosher salt and freshly ground pepper

1 cup (8 fl oz/250 ml) beer or water

1 cup (8 fl oz/250 ml) *crema mexicana**

2 teaspoons chipotles in adobo, chopped

4 cups (32 fl oz/1 l) plus 1 tablespoon peanut or vegetable oil

6 oz (185 g) fresh chorizo sausage

12 taco-size corn tortillas

6 largemouth bass fillets, skin and lateral line removed, cut into strips 3 by 1 inches (7.5 by 2.5 cm)

2 limes, cut into wedges

2 cups (6 oz/185 g) finely shredded green and/or red cabbage

**Crema mexicana* is available at most Latin markets. Many grocery stores stock *crema media,* a slightly sweeter variation. (If using this, add a teaspoon of salt to offset the sweetness.) In a pinch, try sour cream or even crème fraîche.

Mix the egg yolk, flour, 1 teaspoon salt, ½ teaspoon pepper, and the beer together until you have a pancake-like batter. Refrigerate up to 24 hours.

To make a chipotle *crema,* combine the *crema mexicana* with the chipotles—including some adobo sauce—in a food processor until smooth and pinkish.

Heat 1 tablespoon of the oil in a skillet over medium heat. Slice the chorizo lengthwise, peel off the thin casing, and chop. Cook, using a wooden spoon to break the meat into pinto bean–size pieces, until crisp, about 5 minutes. Drain on paper towels.

Preheat the oven to 350°F (180°C). In a large pot or deep fryer, heat the remaining 4 cups oil to 350°F (180°C). While it's heating, whisk the reserved egg white until stiff and fold it into the batter. When the oil is not quite fully heated, wrap the tortillas in foil and place in the oven until soft and warm. Dip the bass in the batter, coating the pieces well. Shake off any excess and fry in batches until crisp and golden brown. Drain on paper towels and lightly salt.

▶ **SERVING TIP** Place 2 or 3 pieces of fish on a warm tortilla. Squeeze lime juice on top, add a few bits of chorizo, and top with cabbage, dollops of salsa (see right), and *crema* to taste. Serve immediately.

ROASTED TOMATILLO-TEQUILA SALSA

1 red bell pepper

1 jalapeño chile

1 lb (500 g) tomatillos, husked and rinsed

1 small white onion, chopped

2 tablespoons cilantro, chopped

½ teaspoon chopped fresh oregano

½ teaspoon salt

1½ teaspoons orange zest

Juice of 2 limes

1 tablespoon tequila, ideally gold or dark

Preheat the broiler. Roast the red bell pepper and jalapeño, turning frequently, until the skins are fully blackened. Place in a zip-seal bag and let rest for 1 minute. Peel, seed, and chop them.

Set the husked tomatillos on a baking sheet 4 inches (10 cm) beneath the broiler heat source. Roast until black splotches appear, about 5 minutes, then turn and repeat on the other side.

While the tomatillos cool, put the chopped peppers and chiles in a bowl, add the remaining ingredients, and stir until everything is evenly incorporated. Chop the cooled tomatillos (or pulse in a food processor), being careful to reserve all the sweet seedy mush that oozes from them, and add to the salsa mixture. Refrigerate until ready to use.

WILD TURKEY ROULADES

Chef Robert Wiedmaier of Washington, D.C., hunts as seriously as he cooks. In this recipe, he extracts a multitude of flavors from a wild turkey by stuffing its breast meat with a sausage made from its dark meat. Serve with roasted Brussels sprouts and roasted fingerling potatoes.

SAUCE

One 20- to 25-lb (10- to 12.5-kg) wild turkey, skinned

8 tablespoons (1 stick/4 oz/125 g) butter

5 shallots, roughly chopped

1 carrot, roughly chopped

2 ribs celery, roughly chopped

4 strips plus ½ lb (250 g) bacon

1 bunch thyme, plus 2 tablespoons thyme leaves

1 bottle Madeira wine

5 cups (40 fl oz/1.25 l) chicken or turkey stock

2 lb (1 kg) cleaned chanterelle mushrooms, cut in half (save trimmings for sauce)

SAUSAGE

4 whole Granny Smith apples, cored and peeled

2 Vidalia onions, roughly chopped

1 head garlic, cloves peeled

2 tablespoons olive oil

½ cup (2 oz/60 g) dried bread crumbs

4 whole eggs

Salt and freshly ground black pepper

2 cups (16 fl oz/500 ml) cream

¼ cup (2 fl oz/60 ml) grainy mustard

MAKE THE SAUCE Remove the turkey breasts and cut off the thighs and wings. Chop the remaining carcass, along with the entire wing bones, into small pieces. Melt the butter in a sauté pan over medium-high heat, and brown the chopped carcass and wings in batches as needed, to prevent crowding. Add the shallots, carrot, celery, 4 strips of the bacon, and the bunch of thyme, and reduce the heat to medium. Cook until golden brown, stirring. Pour in the wine, raise the heat to medium-high, and simmer until the wine is reduced by half. Add the stock and mushroom scraps, and simmer uncovered for 2 hours, skimming any scum from the top.

MAKE THE SAUSAGE Bone the thigh meat; add the bones to the sauce. Using a meat grinder or food processor, grind the thigh meat along with the remaining ½ lb bacon and the apples, onions, and garlic. (If using a grinder, do it twice.) Refrigerate the mixture. Heat the olive oil in a sauté pan over medium-high heat and sauté the chanterelles until golden and softened, then set aside to cool. Add the mushrooms to the sausage along with the bread crumbs, 2 tablespoons thyme leaves, and eggs. Season well with salt and pepper and keep refrigerated.

Lay the turkey breasts on the cutting board and, holding the knife parallel to the board, butterfly the breasts by carefully slicing them through the middle—not all the way though, but just until you can open them like a book. Lay plastic wrap over them and pound to an even thickness, about ½ inch (12 mm). Season with salt and pepper. Scoop half the sausage mixture into each; spread it out evenly, leaving a 1-inch (2.5-cm) border on the edges. Roll the breasts up lengthwise, then tie with butcher's twine in 4 places to maintain the roll. Refrigerate for 1 hour, uncovered.

Strain the sauce, discarding the solids. Return the sauce to a clean saucepan over medium heat and simmer to reduce by half. Add the cream, then continue to reduce by a quarter. Add the mustard, season with salt and pepper, and keep warm.

Preheat oven to 325°F (165°C). While the sauce is reducing, place the turkey roulades on a sheet pan and roast in the oven for about 45 minutes to an hour, until golden brown.

▶ **SERVING TIP** Slice the roulades crosswise and spoon the sauce on top.

MORELS: THE TURKEY HUNTER'S MUSHROOM

Morels—also known as "Molly moochers," "miracles," and "dryland fish"—are America's mushroom, more so than any other. It may be because they're so widespread, they're easy to identify, and they come up in the spring, giving people a reason to get out and enjoy warm weather after a long winter. Or maybe they're popular simply because they taste so good. Morels are so prized that they can sell for up to $50 per pound in some markets.

What follows is a quick guide for finding your own. Always go with an experienced morel hunter and study up to know exactly what you are looking for; there are potentially dangerous mushrooms that resemble morels. That said, here are the basics.

1 TAKE SHAPE Morels are a relatively easy mushroom to identify—and are found in most of the United States from late March through May. In the photo to the left, notice the pits, the distinctive conical shape, and the way the bottom of the cap (the pitted part) is attached near the bottom of the stem.

2 WATCH THE THERMOMETER Morels appear when nighttime lows reach the 40s F (4–9°C) and daytime highs hit the 60s F (15–20°C). Soil temperatures of 50–60°F (10–15°C) provide ideal growing conditions for this easy-to-spot mushroom. Once temps are right, rain triggers morel growth. When daytime highs reach the 80s F (27–32°C), the season ends.

3 LEARN YOUR TREES Certain trees are reliable indicators of morels. In much of the morel's range, dead elms (with the bark slipping off) or apple trees—even apple tree stumps—mark a likely spot. Look around white ash and tulip poplars in the South. In the Mountain West, morels typically grow among Douglas firs. Early in the spring, as the ground is warming, you'll find them on south-facing slopes in fairly open areas. As the season progresses, go deeper into the woods and onto north-facing slopes.

4 SEARCH TWEETS Here's a sneaky trick. Use Twitter's search feature to find keywords in tweets from the area you want to scout. Morel hunters usually won't divulge their top-secret mushroom locations, but you can figure out where and when people are finding morels.

5 FIND THE PATTERN—OR FOLLOW THE FIRE The woods are full of microclimates. Think of morel hunting like bass fishing: You cover ground until you find one, then you focus on similar areas—elevations, contours, exposures—as you hunt. Also, the years after a fire can be banner. Keep an eye out for brush fires or controlled burns in your area. —P.B.

MOREL CREAM SAUCE

Don't let hot, wet, dry, or stormy spring weather keep you out of the woods, eyes glued to the ground in search of spring's fungal bounty: morels. A few warm days will get the dogwoods blooming, turkeys gobbling, and morels growing, reminding me of why I love spring and adding a little foraging to my outdoor regimen.

It's hard to beat the simple savory flavor of morels sautéed in butter, but there are a number of ways to put nature's bounty to work in the kitchen. A terrific option is to make a fairly simple mushroom cream sauce that can be used to top wild turkey breasts, venison steaks, or even pasta.

First, soak the morels in water for an hour or 2 to clean them and wash out any bugs living inside the hollow pits. For a more thorough cleaning, slice the mushrooms lengthwise, then cover with water.

Next, in a medium skillet, sauté about a dozen morels, along with 2 cloves of minced garlic in a few tablespoons of butter. Throw in a generous pinch of salt.

After about 5 minutes, lower the heat and splash in a little dry white wine to deglaze the pan, letting it reduce by about half. (Don't forget to splash a little in a glass for yourself.)

Off the heat, slowly whisk in ½ cup heavy cream and about a cup of venison stock (or, in a pinch, chicken stock).

If the sauce is a little thick, add more stock. If it's too thin, put it back on the stovetop and gently simmer to thicken.

Add some tarragon or rosemary, depending on your preference. Salt and pepper to taste. —D.D.

TURKEY SOUP WITH MORELS, SPRING PEAS & ASPARAGUS

A spring soup is a great way to use the dark meat left over after you breast out a gobbler, plus any morels you forage along the way. Classic spring vegetables round out this homage to the season.

SERVES 4

1 wild turkey carcass with legs and thighs, skinned

1 large yellow onion, roughly chopped

4 carrots, roughly chopped

4 ribs celery, roughly chopped

Salt and freshly ground black pepper

2 cups (16 fl oz/500 ml) chicken stock

2 bay leaves

2 tablespoons unsalted butter

2 oz (60 g) fresh morel mushrooms or 1 ounce dried, softened in boiling water for 20 minutes

1 teaspoon fresh thyme leaves

1 bunch asparagus, trimmed of woody ends and chopped into 1-inch (2.5-cm) lengths

⅓ cup (1½ oz/45 g) fresh or frozen peas

1 tablespoon chopped fresh tarragon

Preheat the oven to 450°F (230°C). Roughly hack the turkey carcass until you have pieces that will fit into a pot, and place them in a roasting pan along with the onion, carrots, and celery. Add salt and pepper, then roast until the turkey and vegetables are well browned but not blackened, about 1 hour.

Transfer the pan's contents into a large pot. Add the stock, bay leaves, and enough cold water to cover. Bring to a simmer and cook over very low heat, uncovered, until the thigh meat is very tender and the liquid is flavorful, at least 3 hours (the longer the simmer, the more intense the flavors). Occasionally skim the scum from the surface. Remove the turkey pieces and let cool. Strain the liquid through a colander into another pot and discard the vegetables. (You will need 5 cups/40 fl oz/1.25 l liquid for the soup; refrigerate or freeze the remainder.) Pick the meat off the bones, then discard the bones. (Everything, to this point, can be done in advance. Refrigerate the liquid and meat until ready to use.)

Bring the 5 cups of liquid to a simmer. While it's heating, melt the butter in a small sauté pan over medium-low heat. Add the mushrooms and thyme, and sauté gently until soft, about 8 minutes. Add the asparagus, peas, and reserved turkey meat to the liquid, and simmer for 5 minutes, or until the asparagus is just tender and the meat is warmed through. Taste and adjust the seasoning.

▶ **SERVING TIP** Divide the soup among 4 bowls. Divide the morels among the bowls and garnish with the chopped tarragon.

BRAISED BEAR SHANKS

Due to the amount of sinew that bear shanks are laced with, they need to be cooked low and slow. You can use the same recipe in the fall for venison shanks.

SERVES 4–6

2 tablespoons vegetable oil

2 bear shanks, cut into 2 pieces each

Kosher salt and freshly ground black pepper

¼ cup (1½ oz/45 g) all-purpose flour

1 yellow onion, chopped

2 ribs celery, chopped

4 cloves garlic, minced

¼ cup (2 fl oz/60 ml) red wine

2–3 cups (16–24 fl oz/500–750 ml) beef or game stock

1 cup (3 oz/90 g) sliced mushrooms

Preheat the oven to 300°F (150°C). Heat the oil in a large pot or Dutch oven over medium-high heat. Pat the bear shanks dry with paper towels and liberally season them with salt, then dust with flour.

When the oil is just to the point of smoking, add the bear shanks in batches, to avoid crowding. Brown the shanks 5–6 minutes, turning them every few minutes so each side gets nice and brown. Transfer to a plate and lower the heat to medium.

Dump the onion, celery, and garlic into the pot and stir. Sauté until the onions turn translucent, 3–5 minutes. (I like to add another pinch or two of salt and lots of black pepper at this step, too.)

Deglaze the pot with a few glugs of red wine, scraping loose any tasty brown bits from the bottom. Simmer for a few minutes until the wine is reduced by half.

Return the bear shanks to the Dutch oven and pour in stock until it reaches about halfway up the meat. Cover, put in the oven, and cook for 3 hours, adding mushrooms and lots of fresh, cracked black pepper for the last 30–45 minutes.

(If the pan sauce seems too thin, reduce it on the stovetop or add a slurry of 1 tablespoon cornstarch mixed with 1 tablespoon water or stock, and bring to a boil.) Serve the shanks with the sauce. —D.D.

HOW TO RENDER BEAR FAT

The hard, white lard from a bear is a great medium for frying. Nothing beats onions and potatoes poached in bear fat—except maybe chicken thighs dusted with seasoned flour. Rendering bear fat is easy but time-consuming; luckily, this process involves mostly unattended cooking, just a stir every now and then to keep the pieces from sticking to the pan. Do it outdoors—bear fat can be smelly.

1 Clean the fat thoroughly, removing any stray fur and cutting away as much as possible. Cut the fat into 1-inch (2.5-cm) squares and add to a deep stockpot. (The deeper the pot, the better, as grease can splatter.)

2 Set the pot over medium-low heat, and stir regularly at first to keep the fat from sticking. (A bit of water added to the pot can also help prevent scorching.) You want the fat to sputter, but not sizzle and turn brown, so keep the heat low.

3 Let the fat render and moisture evaporate. Depending on the amount of fat, this could take several hours or all day. Be sure to stir a few times every hour.

4 When the fat is completely liquefied and has stopped sputtering, you're done. There will be a few hard bits of fat—cracklings—that you'll filter out. Line a fine-meshed sieve with cheesecloth and set it over a bowl. Slowly pour the rendered fat through the sieve to filter out the cracklings and impurities.

5 Transfer the fat to jars, seal, and refrigerate. Bear fat should last several months in the fridge and even longer if frozen. —D.D.

GREEN CHILE VENISON STEW WITH APACHE BREAD

Here's a flavorful and simple stew inspired by the Native American cooking of the Southwest. The marriage of mild chiles and venison is a classic one, and this is especially good with Apache bread—cornmeal and bacon fat, roasted in a corn husk—crumbled on top. If you're in the Southwest, use the best green chiles you can find. For the rest of us, the canned variety sold in most grocery stores will suffice just fine; figure on four 7-ounce (220-g) cans, and drain the chiles before adding them to the stew.

SERVES 4–6

APACHE BREAD
8 dried corn husks*

¾ cup (5 oz/155 g) white cornmeal

¾ cup (5 oz/155 g) yellow cornmeal

Salt and freshly ground black pepper

¾ cup (6 fl oz/180 ml) boiling water

¼ cup (2 fl oz/60 ml) plus 1 tablespoon bacon drippings

STEW
2 lb (1 kg) venison, cut into 1-inch (2.5-cm) cubes

¼ cup (2 fl oz/60 ml) vegetable oil, or as needed

2 yellow onions, diced

1 tablespoon minced garlic

2 bay leaves

6 cups (48 fl oz/1.5 l) chicken stock

3 cups (24 oz/750 g) roasted, peeled, and chopped green chiles

1 red bell pepper, seeded and diced

2 tablespoons finely chopped cilantro

*Corn husks are available at many grocery stores and Latin markets.

MAKE THE APACHE BREAD Soak the dried corn husks in water until soft and pliable, about 30 minutes. Preheat the oven to 350°F (180°C). Combine the white and yellow cornmeals in a medium bowl with a generous sprinkling of salt and pepper, then add the boiling water and bacon drippings, and stir with a wooden spoon until a dough forms. Using your hands, form the dough into 8 fat cylinders, then wrap these with the corn husks, tying the ends with kitchen twine. Place the filled husks on a baking sheet and bake for 1 hour.

MAKE THE STEW Pat the meat dry with paper towels, and salt and pepper it generously. Heat the oil in a Dutch oven over high heat, and brown the meat in batches, so as not to crowd the pot. (Add additional oil, if necessary.) Remove the meat with a slotted spoon and set aside.

You should have about 3 tablespoons oil left in the pan; add more if needed. Add the onions, reduce the heat to medium, and sauté until limp and golden; then stir in the garlic and sauté for 1 minute. Return the meat, and any juices, to the pot, then add the bay leaves and chicken stock, and bring to a boil.

Reduce the heat to low and skim any foam from the surface. Simmer, covered, for 1 hour, then remove the cover and simmer for 30 minutes more. Add the chiles and bell pepper, and cook for 15 minutes, then add the cilantro, and salt and pepper to taste.

Remove the Apache bread from the husks and serve warm on the side.

TROUT ON A NAIL

Here's a primitive but fantastic way to "grill" a fish, straight from Finland: Butterfly it, then nail it to a board and cook it by the reflected heat of a campfire. The meat derives flavor from the wood smoke as well as from the blackening board onto which it's nailed. Even better? There's no pan to clean.

SERVES 2

1 trout, about 2 lb (1 kg)

4 tablespoons (2 oz/60 g) butter, melted

1 tablespoon brown sugar

1 tablespoon dry mustard

1 tablespoon sweet paprika

Coarse salt and freshly ground black pepper

Dill sprigs and lemon wedges for garnish

Special equipment: untreated oak, hickory, cedar, or other hardwood plank, ideally about 10 inches (25 cm) wide and 3 feet (90 cm) long

After making a good, hot campfire, prepare the trout. Split the trout through the back or the belly (splitting a fish from the back is generally easier) so that it opens like a book. Remove the backbone and viscera. Rinse the trout, inside and out, under cold water, then dry with paper towels.

Brush the skin side with some of the melted butter. Then nail the trout, skin side down, to an untreated oak, hickory, cedar, or other hardwood plank. Six nails should do the trick. Be sure not to pound the nails all the way in—you'll be pulling them out soon enough.

Combine the sugar, mustard, paprika, and salt and pepper to taste in a small bowl. Brush the trout with some of the remaining melted butter, and sprinkle the spice mixture onto the flesh, patting gently.

Make sure your campfire is roaring hot. In this situation, unlike most campfire-cooking scenarios, flames are helpful. Stand the board 12–18 inches (30–45 cm) from the fire, with the head of the trout at the bottom; prop it upright with a few sticks. The trout will cook from the reflected heat of the campfire in about 15–20 minutes. Check for doneness by flicking the meat with a fingertip to see if it flakes.

When the fish is cooked, remove the nails and transfer the fish to a plate. Garnish with sprigs of dill and serve with lemon wedges.

WILD TURKEY SCALLOPS WITH BABY ARTICHOKES & LEMON

Quick sautéing is a cooking method well suited to ultra-lean wild turkey breast, which can easily get dry if you overcook it. A buttery lemon pan sauce adds a velvety burst of flavor.

SERVES 4

Juice of 1 lemon, plus 3 tablespoons lemon juice

16 baby artichokes

About 1 cup (5 oz/155 g) all-purpose flour

Salt and freshly ground black pepper

1½ lb (750 g) wild turkey breast, cut into roughly ½-inch (12-mm) slices

¼ cup (2 fl oz/60 ml) plus 2 tablespoons olive oil

3 tablespoons unsalted butter

1 cup (8 fl oz/250 ml) chicken stock

3 cloves garlic, minced

1 teaspoon red pepper flakes

PREP THE ARTICHOKES Prepare an ice-water bath in a large nonaluminum bowl. Add the juice of 1 lemon. Peel and discard the outer leaves of each artichoke until you reach the tender center. Lop off the tops and bottoms, and quarter the artichoke lengthwise. (If there's any fuzzy choke, scoop it out with a paring knife.) Immediately add the artichoke quarters to the ice water, and proceed to the next. Reserve in the water until ready to cook.

PREP AND COOK THE TURKEY Put the flour in a shallow bowl and season generously with salt and pepper. Place a slice of turkey breast between two sheets of plastic wrap. With the flat side of a meat mallet, pound the meat until it is ⅛- to ¼-inch (3- to 6-mm) thick. (You can also use a cast iron skillet or a rolling pin for this.) Transfer the pounded turkey to the flour for dredging, shake off the excess, and place on a wire rack or sheet pan while you repeat the process with the remaining turkey slices.

Preheat the oven to 200°F (95°C). In a large, heavy skillet, heat 2 tablespoons of the olive oil and 2 tablespoons of the butter over medium-high heat. Add the turkey scallops to the pan, in batches, and cook until deliciously golden brown, about 1½ minutes per side. (Cut through one to check for doneness—slightly pink is okay.) As the turkey scallops are cooked, transfer them to a sheet pan and place in the oven to keep warm.

When all of the turkey is cooked, add the remaining 3 tablespoons lemon juice and the chicken stock to the skillet. Scrape up the browned bits on the bottom of the pan with a wooden spoon. Bring to a boil, and continue to cook until the liquid has reduced to a sauce-like consistency. Remove from the heat and strain into a small saucepan.

COOK THE ARTICHOKES Drain the artichokes and pat dry with paper towels. Heat the remaining ¼ cup olive oil in a large sauté pan over medium-high heat. Add the artichokes to the hot oil and cook, stirring occasionally, until golden brown and tender, about 6 minutes. Add the garlic, red pepper flakes, and salt and pepper to taste, and continue to cook, about another minute. Meanwhile, place the sauce over medium heat and bring to a simmer. Stir in the remaining 1 tablespoon butter.

To serve, divide the artichokes among 4 plates. Divide the turkey scallops, and spoon the sauce over the turkey. Pass extra sauce around the table.

FIX THE PERFECT SHORE LUNCH

Shore lunch, the fisherman's feast cooked and eaten riverside, is the epitome of outdoor dining, and any angler worth his weight in cast iron has his own idea of what makes the best midday meal. A true shore lunch is fish and fried, crispy potatoes. Add a side of corn or beans, and you have a perfect break during a long day on the water. Here are a few tips to help you enjoy shore lunch at its finest. Just remember, no shore lunch is complete without a post-feast nap.

FRY THE FISH

You fish. You fry. This is the ritual of the river trip, and here is how you get from a cooler full of fish to a riverbank feast. At home, fill a Nalgene bottle with peanut oil. Pour 2 cups of breading mix into a 1-gallon, zip-seal bag. Stuff it—along with a second empty bag, coffee filters, paper towels, and a baggie of Cajun spice mix—into a second plastic water bottle. Your fry kit is complete. At the shore-side cook site, it'll be quick and easy to put it all together.

1 Pour enough peanut oil into a skillet to cover the fillets' sides but not spill over their tops. Build a fire between two long parallel logs and place the skillet on them. You don't need coals. For precise flame control, keep smaller branches handy.

2 Season the fillets liberally with Cajun spice and toss them into the empty bag. Shake well. Add bread crumbs and, using your fingers, work the breading into the cracks. Shake off the excess. Now get ready—here comes the magic.

3 The oil should be almost smoking hot. Ease in a small piece of test fish. You want a rolling, sputtering boil around the edges. Nothing less will do. Gently add the other pieces, but don't crowd the pan.

4 Give the fillets 2 to 5 minutes per side. When the fish turns the color of caramel, turn carefully—and only once. It's done when you can flake the fillet all the way through. Drain fillets on paper towels. Let the excess oil cool and strain it back into its bottle using a coffee filter to reuse. —T.E.N.

THE COOLER COMMANDMENTS

Here's how to pack a better (and safer) summer meal:

1 A full cooler is more efficient than an empty one.

2 Bacteria thrive in moist conditions. Place a drip tray at the bottom and cover it with a wire rack.

3 Use an adequate amount of ice or frozen gel packs to maintain temperatures below 40 degrees.

4 Limit the number of times you lift the lid, and keep visits short by listing the contents outside.

5 Store sandwich toppings in separate containers so bread doesn't become soggy.

6 Cold air sinks. Stack frozen steaks, chops, and chicken breasts near the top, but make sure the raw meat is fully sealed. —D.D.

CRISP THE POTATOES

You'll want to bring along some spuds that you've already cooked—otherwise lunch will take a lot longer to fix, leaving less time to get back to fishing.

WHAT YOU'LL NEED
2 pounds (1 kg) cooked potatoes
4 strips bacon, diced
1 large yellow onion, chopped
Salt and pepper to taste

TO PREPARE Dice the potatoes into 1-inch (2.5-cm) chunks. In a large skillet, over medium-high heat, sauté the bacon. Once the fat begins to render out, add the onion. Cook until the onions are shiny and soft (about 5 minutes), stirring often. Add the potatoes and cook 8–10 minutes, then cover and cook another 5 minutes. Season with salt and pepper. —T.E.N.

FOR A LIGHTER LUNCH

WRAP IT Stuff a cleaned trout with lemon slices and fresh dill. Seal it all tightly in tinfoil coated on the inside with butter. Cook directly on hot coals.

GRILL IT Slash each side of a whole fish 3 or 4 times with a knife. Coat with olive oil, salt, and pepper. Fill cavity with fresh herbs. Grill over a hot flame. —D.D.

PANFISH CHOWDER

Here's a recipe for one of those lazy, sun-dappled spring days when the breeze is blowing and the bream have been happily bending a cane pole for hours. It's a classic fish chowder that gets some extra warm-weather sweetness from its "corn stock" base, made by simmering the cobs. This is a superb use for panfish, but you can substitute almost any other fish (or even shrimp or oysters) with equally satisfying results.

SERVES 4

4 large ears fresh corn

2 tablespoons vegetable oil

1 yellow onion, coarsely chopped

2 carrots, peeled and coarsely chopped

2 ribs celery, coarsely chopped

4 whole peppercorns

¼ lb (125 g) bacon, diced

2 russet potatoes, peeled and cut into ½-inch (12-mm) cubes

Salt and freshly ground black pepper

1½ lb (750 g) panfish fillets, cut into 2-inch (5-cm) pieces

½ cup (4 fl oz/125 ml) heavy cream

2 tablespoons chopped Italian parsley

First, make a corn stock. Cut the kernels from the corn and set them aside. (A great method: Use a Bundt cake pan. Place the tip of the cob in the pan's center hole to steady it, and slice the kernels off into the pan with a knife.) Snap the cobs in half. Heat the vegetable oil in a large stockpot over medium-high heat, then add the onion, carrots, celery, and peppercorns. Cook, stirring frequently, until the onion is translucent and bronzed on the edges, about 8 minutes. Add the halved cobs and 8 cups (64 fl oz/2 l) cold water. Bring the mixture to a boil, then reduce the heat to low and simmer for 40 minutes. Set a colander over another pot and strain the stock. Toss out the vegetables.

In a large pot or Dutch oven over medium heat, sauté the bacon until almost, but not quite, crispy. Remove with a slotted spoon and set aside to drain on paper towels. Add the potatoes and reserved corn kernels to the pot, along with generous dashes of salt and pepper, and sauté, stirring, for 5 minutes. Add the corn stock and bring to a boil; simmer for 12 minutes, or until the potatoes are almost tender. Gently drop the pieces of fish into the mixture. Cover the pot and cook for an additional 3 minutes, or until the fish is just cooked through. Add the cream by pouring it carefully around the sides of the pot, then shaking the pot to incorporate it. (You don't want to stir, lest you break up the fish.)

▶ **SERVING TIP** Ladle into bowls, garnish with the chopped parsley, and serve. Try experimenting with different types of bacon to vary the flavor. For example, you can use peppered bacon, applewood-smoked bacon, corn cob–smoked bacon (a New England staple), or Canadian bacon.

SUMMER

"Summer afternoon—summer afternoon," wrote the novelist Henry James. "To me those have always been the two most beautiful words in the English language."

For many of us, summer afternoons were the seedbeds for our outdoor pursuits. Summer afternoons were when, as children, we carried cane poles or spincasting combos to the closest water and let bluegills tear apart our bait and, occasionally, allow themselves to be hooked on our lines. If hours could pass more enjoyably we couldn't imagine how. And though our gear has grown up, along with the size and variety of the fish we pursue, in many ways we ourselves haven't: One of our simplest but deepest pleasures remains casting beneath a big yellow summer sun, the unnoticed hours slipping past us.

For cooks, too, the living is easy: the backyard grill welcomes everything we bring to it. If there's venison left in the deep-freeze, its best use is in burgers, hand-mixed with ground pork and grilled to juicy charred perfection. Summer is fish-fry season, too, the time for anglers to gather around a vat of bubbling oil, often with beer in hand, to witness their breaded catch transformed by the fryer into golden treasure.

Summer makes no demands on us: "In summer," a poet once wrote, "the song sings itself." And while the fish don't catch themselves, nor do the meals make themselves, on the best summer afternoons it can often feel that way.

VENISON SLIDERS

This ground mixture can be used to make regular-size burgers, but sliders always go fast at parties and tailgates. Just double or triple the mixture as needed. Since venison is so lean, the addition of pork ensures a juicy burger. As for the fixings, the ones suggested here stand up nicely to venison, but don't feel wedded to them. The best burger is the one you make your own.

MAKES 8 SLIDERS

½ lb (250 g) ground venison

½ lb (250 g) ground pork

Salt and freshly ground black pepper

8 slider buns or mini potato rolls

4 oz (125 g) blue cheese, crumbled

Bread and butter pickles for garnish

Thinly sliced small inner red onion rings for garnish

Prepare a medium-hot fire (375°F/190°C) in a grill. Use damp, cool fingertips or a fork to mix the venison and pork, season well with salt and pepper, then form into 8 small equal-size patties. Be careful not to overwork the meat.

Oil the grill and grill the patties just to medium doneness, 3–4 minutes on the first side and about 2 minutes on the second side. Remove the patties to a plate and briefly grill the cut sides of the buns, just until browned. Serve the sliders on the grilled buns with crumbled blue cheese, bread and butter pickles, and onion rings on top. —S.P.C.

TIPS FOR GRINDING BETTER VENISON

No meat sold at the market is more local, humanely raised, drug free, and genetically unmodified than that from a wild animal cleanly killed. Here are some tips to get the best from your burger.

BUY THE BEST GRINDER YOU CAN AFFORD An underpowered grinder, or one with a dull knife, won't grind meat cleanly. If the meat coming from the grinder plate looks like it's been extruded rather than cut, make sure the back of the plate is free from sinew and the retaining ring is on tight.

YOU GET OUT WHAT YOU PUT IN Who knows what ground meat from the grocer contains. Do it yourself and control the final product. Make sure you clean your meat well and trim sinew, yellow fat, silverskin, and all bloodshot meat with a judicious, keen hand.

KEEP THINGS COLD You'll get a much better grind if your meat and machine are cold. Put cubed meat in the freezer for 30 minutes until it's firm to the touch. Throw the grinder neck, auger, blades, and plate in there as well.

DON'T FORGET FAT Beef has fat built right in, but wild game needs a boost. You can use several things to up the fat content and flavor, like bacon trimmings, which add a distinctive flavor to burgers and meat loaf, or beef tallow and pork butt (both available from butchers). You can control the ratio, but I like 10 to 15 percent. You can also supplement with eggs or bread crumbs soaked in milk. Either way, you'll need some kind of moisture to avoid a crumbly burger. —D.D.

JALAPEÑO TARTAR SAUCE

½ cup (2 oz/60 g) pickle chips

¼ cup (1 oz/30 g) chopped onion

2 tablespoons capers

1 fresh garlic clove

2 cups (16 fl oz/500 ml) mayonnaise

2 tablespoons Dijon mustard

1½ teaspoons lemon juice

1 scant teaspoon lemon zest

½ teaspoon black pepper

½ teaspoon dried dill

½ teaspoon sugar

½ cup (4 oz/125 g) jalapeño chiles, seeded and finely diced

Try this version of the classic tartar sauce for a grown-up fish dip. The fresh flavor of the chiles is a clean, zesty addition to the citrus, and pairs nicely. Finely chop the pickle chips, onion, capers, and garlic in a food processor. Drain the liquid, then add the mixture to the mayonnaise in a mixing bowl. Add the mustard, lemon juice, lemon zest, pepper, dill, and sugar. Whisk thoroughly, until smoothly incorporated. Add the jalapeños, seeded and finely diced, and whisk again. Serve and enjoy.

THE LAKE ERIE MONSTER

The most outlandish grilled-cheese sandwich I've ever encountered is called the Lake Erie Monster, from Melt Bar & Grilled in Cleveland, in which a Guinness-battered walleye fillet is swamped in a gleeful mess of melted cheese, jammed between thick slices of toast, and served with jalapeño-spiked tartar sauce. This is fish-camp cuisine taken to its belt-loosening outer limits.

SERVES 4

BATTER

¾ cup (4 oz/125 g) all-purpose flour, plus ½ cup (2½ oz/75 g)

1 teaspoon kosher salt

½ teaspoon black pepper

¼ teaspoon chili powder

¼ teaspoon baking powder

3 eggs

½ cup (4 fl oz/125 ml) Guinness stout

¼ cup (2 fl oz/60 ml) buttermilk

Oil for frying

4 walleye fillets (or other firm white-fleshed fish)

8 slices thick white bread (such as Texas Toast), toasted

16 slices American cheese

Jalapeño Tartar Sauce (at left)

MAKE THE BATTER In a large bowl, whisk together ¾ cup (4 oz/125 g) of the flour with the salt, pepper, chili powder, and baking powder. In a smaller bowl, whisk the eggs, beer, and buttermilk until combined. Pour the wet ingredients into the larger bowl and whisk until smooth.

FRY THE FISH Preheat the oven to 375°F (190°C). Heat the oil in a deep fryer or heavy pot to 350°F (180°C). Rinse the walleye fillets in cold water, then pat dry with paper towels. Spread the remaining flour on a plate and dredge the fillets in it, shaking off any excess. When the oil is ready, dip the floured fillets in the batter one at a time, fully coating each so the batter is thick and drippy. Add to the oil, and continue with the remaining fillets. Fry until the fish is cooked through and golden brown, 7–10 minutes.

MAKE THE SANDWICH While the fish is cooking, arrange the toasted bread slices on a baking sheet and place 2 slices of cheese on each one. When the fish is done, move the fillets to a paper towel to absorb excess oil, then place atop the cheese on 4 slices of bread. Place in the oven for about 3 minutes, or until the cheese is melted and bubbly. Remove from the oven, and construct the sandwiches. Serve with jalapeño tartar sauce.

ESSENTIAL CAMP KITCHEN GEAR

What you won't find here are any cleanup supplies. Why? Because if you're cooking at camp, dish duty isn't your problem.

TINDER TABS When you're hungry, you want that fire built as fast as possible, so some synthetic assistance doesn't hurt.

DO-IT-ALL KNIFE No cleaver or paring knife here, so bring a sharp, trusty folder that can handle all of the cutting.

FILLET KNIFE Except for the fish, that is. For that, you'll need to bring along a small fillet knife.

CUTTING BOARDS Have at least two—one for meat and fish and one for everything else.

STOVE You'll want two burners to cook more at once; a cooking surface big enough for a large pot and pan; and a durable case to protect it on those bumpy dirt roads.

POTS Go with a nonstick coating for a smoother cleanup, and a fitted lid with a built-in strainer makes draining water much easier.

FRY PAN If weight and space are a concern, use a light nonstick pan with a folding handle. Otherwise, stick with the camp classic: cast iron.

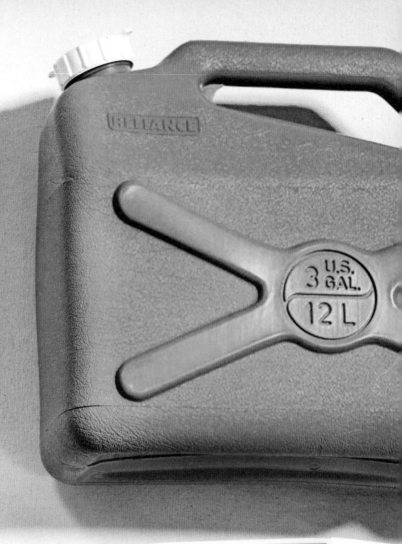

UTENSIL SET The wildest wild chefs can make do with their camp knife and a stick, but there's no shame in bringing your own flatware. Bonus points if you pack a spork.

WATER JUG Think of this as your camp sink. Refill it whenever you can, because it'll empty fast.

COOLER Make sure you follow the "Cooler Commandments," on page 166.

COFFEE SET The life of an outdoorsman demands early wake-up calls. Coffee helps.

SALMON KEBABS WITH HORSERADISH BUTTER

An easy campfire meal for your next fishing trip, you can boost the flavor of these campfire-charred salmon kebabs by using green twigs rather than store-bought skewers. Just sharpen one end of the twigs with a pocketknife and shave off the bark. Cedar or alder is especially recommended for salmon—as is horseradish butter.

HORSERADISH BUTTER

1 inch (2.5 cm) fresh horseradish root, peeled

8 tablespoons (1 stick/4 oz/125 g) unsalted butter, at room temperature

1 teaspoon apple cider vinegar

½ teaspoon brown sugar

½ teaspoon salt

POTATOES

20 small red-skinned potatoes

4 sprigs fresh rosemary

4 cloves garlic, peeled

12 shallots or pearl onions, immersed in boiling water for 2 minutes, then peeled by slicing off the root end and squeezing out the onion

4 tablespoons (2 fl oz/60 ml) olive oil

Salt and freshly ground black pepper

2 lb (1 kg) salmon fillet, cut into 1½-inch (4-cm) chunks (any firm, meaty fish will work)

MAKE THE HORSERADISH BUTTER To make this streamside, prepare the butter and potatoes at home in advance. Grate the horseradish root and mix it well with the butter, vinegar, sugar, and salt. (Alternately, you can skip the grating step and combine all the ingredients in a food processor fitted with a metal blade. Process until smooth.) Spoon the mixture onto some plastic wrap and cover, twisting the ends to form a tight cylinder. (This will make it easy to transport.) Keep it cold until ready to use.

MAKE THE POTATOES Start with four 12-by-12-inch (30-by-30-cm) sheets of aluminum foil. On each piece, place 5 potatoes, 1 rosemary sprig, 1 garlic clove, and 3 shallots; drizzle with a tablespoon of oil; and salt and pepper generously. Wrap the piles tightly with the foil, adding one or two additional sheets to fully seal the packets. Keep cold until ready to use.

Once streamside, prepare a campfire, allowing a solid bed of hot coals to develop before cooking. (You can also use a grill with a medium-hot fire, 375°F/190°C.) Put the potato packets on the edge of the coals and cook for 25 minutes, turning frequently. Thread the salmon onto the skewers, leaving plenty of room at the ends, and salt and pepper to taste. When the potatoes are about halfway done, make a bed of hot coals and arrange two stones, roughly the size of bricks, on either side of the coals, close enough for the ends of the skewers to be able to rest upon them. Set the skewers so that the salmon chunks are suspended above the coals for about 5 minutes per side, until they're nicely browned and just cooked through.

▶ **SERVING TIP** Slide the fish off the skewers and top with dollops of horseradish butter. Accompany with the potatoes.

GRILLED VENISON BACKSTRAP WITH DEER RUB

The backstrap is the true trophy of a deer, so saving one until summer takes some willpower. But it's worth the wait. Because while fall and winter are for roasting and stewing, summer is for grilling—and grilled venison is a beautiful thing. This backstrap meal, from hunter-chef Tim Love of Lonesome Dove Western Bistro in Forth Worth, is crazy simple—which is a big reason it's so damn good.

SERVES 4

DEER RUB
2 tablespoons cumin
2 tablespoons coriander
1 tablespoon palm sugar
1 tablespoon pure chili powder
1 tablespoon kosher salt

BACKSTRAP
1 large backstrap (venison loin), silverskin removed
½ cup (4 fl oz/125 ml) peanut oil

MAKE THE DEER RUB Combine all the ingredients and stir to mix well.

MAKE THE BACKSTRAP Let the backstrap reach room temperature. Rub with peanut oil. Coat with the deer rub, rubbing the spices well into the meat.

Heat a grill (or grill pan) to 400°F (200°C). Sear the venison for 3 minutes per side.

Remove from grill and let rest for at least 10 minutes. Place back on grill until hot, cut into thin slices and serve. —C.K.

A TRIBUTE TO THE VAUNTED BACKSTRAP

Sure, the tenderloins may be a more immediate delicacy, but they are a fleeting pleasure, small and flirtatious and destined to leave you wanting more. It is the *longissimus dorsi* muscle—the backstrap—that aids the deer in its soaring bounds and its zero-to-see-ya-later speeds, not to mention its edibility. The backstrap is something to behold, and don't forget it.

The backstraps lie just to the sides of the transverse processes of the vertebrae. They are easily freed of gristle and connective tissue and are perhaps the leanest meat on the carcass. They can be removed with a paring knife and cut with a fork. Like good rice or stone-ground grits, backstraps are both step-side pickup and Lamborghini Murciélago. They can stand alone on a plate, seasoned with little more than a touch of flame and a sprinkle of pepper, or they can serve as a canvas for individual expression.

Every serious deer hunter has a secret preparation—a coveted recipe handed down from father to son or stumbled upon due to just enough beer to make you forget the strictures of culinary decency. I've had backstrap slathered in mustard and Coca-Cola, split like a pig and stuffed with tomatoes, and stewed with onions by a Cajun spiritualist.

And each time, it was delicious. I've also had bad backstrap many times, but the sin was always the same—overcooking. Do with the backstrap what you will, but serve it as rare as you can get away with. Then you can eat in one sitting as much backstrap as a single human being can stand. But never so much that you're not left wanting more. —T.E.N.

HOW TO BLEED A BLUEFISH

Though you'd have a hard time finding an angler who doesn't like a good fight with a bluefish, its edibility is often hotly debated. Some people love the taste, others can't stand it. Still others think it's not worth the trouble. I personally only eat bluefish weighing 5 pounds or less, because the bigger they grow, the more oily they get—and they're an oily fish to begin with. Aim small, but regardless of the fish's size, blues should be eaten the same day they're caught. The reason? They don't freeze well. More important, the frequently oily flavor of bluefish can be lessened with a fairly simple and easy trick— at least, it's simple and easy once you get the hang of it. The trick is bleeding the fish and removing the dark bloodlines on the flanks.

As soon as a keeper bluefish is unhooked, use wire cutters to clip the white ribs of one or two gills on just one side of the head. Then place the fish headfirst into a bucket of saltwater so it can still breathe. You want the fish to pump out all of its blood naturally, so keep changing the water until it's no longer turning deep red. It will do the rest of the work for you.

Ice the fish after bleeding. Later, when the fillets have been removed and skinned, make shallow angled V cuts down each side of the dark bloodlines, and peel them away.
—J.C.

THE MONTAUK BURGER

From the easternmost point on Long Island comes this way to cook one of the ocean's most underappreciated gamefish: bluefish burgers. If you can't get bluefish, try mackerel. This is excellent served with grilled corn and chunks of grilled, Old Bay-rubbed potatoes.

SERVES 4

1 large egg, beaten

3 tablespoons mayonnaise

Salt and freshly ground black pepper

2 teaspoons plus 2 tablespoons Old Bay seasoning

2 tablespoons finely chopped Italian parsley

8 no-salt saltine crackers

1 lb (500 g) fresh bluefish fillets, chopped into ½-inch (12-mm) chunks, or other firm, white-fleshed fish

1 lb (500 g) potatoes

3 tablespoons olive oil

4 ears fresh sweet corn

4 tablespoons (2 fl oz/60 ml) melted butter

¼ cup (2 fl oz/60 ml) canola oil, for frying

4 white rolls or small hamburger buns

4 tomato slices

Tartar sauce for serving

Mix the egg, mayonnaise, 1 teaspoon salt, 2 teaspoons Old Bay, and the parsley in a medium bowl. Add 4 crumbled saltine crackers and combine well. Gently fold in the fish and form 4 equal-size patties. Refrigerate them on wax paper (they'll be loose and wet) for at least an hour.

Meanwhile, slice the potatoes ⅜ inch (1 cm) thick and put in a pot with enough cold water to cover. Bring to a boil, then lower the heat and simmer for about 5 minutes, stopping before they are fully cooked. Drain and run under cold water until the potatoes are cool. In a large bowl, pour the olive oil over them and add the remaining 2 tablespoons Old Bay. Stir and set aside.

Prepare a medium-hot fire (375°F/190°C) in your grill. Remove the husks and silk, then cook the corn on the grill, turning frequently, until the tips of the kernels are blackened and the corn is done. Brush with the melted butter and wrap them in foil to keep warm. Grill the potato slices on a tray or tinfoil for about 4 minutes per side, until golden brown and crisp.

Crumble the remaining 4 crackers and gently coat the fish patties on all sides. Heat the canola oil in a skillet over medium heat. Add the patties and fry them to a deep golden brown, about 2–3 minutes per side. (Don't fiddle with them or they'll fall apart.) Put a patty on each roll with a tomato slice and, if desired, tartar sauce.

DECKSIDE CEVICHE

Forget about packing a lunch for your next saltwater fishing trip—you're catching lunch. Ceviche (seh-VEE-chay) is a South American staple in which chunks of very fresh, raw fish are marinated in lime and/or other citrus juices, then tossed with a wide variety of ingredients—onions, peppers, and tropical herbs, typically—into a salsa-like mixture that makes for a dazzlingly refreshing lunch. Sushi-phobes, relax: The acid in the citrus firms up the fish, so that, while still technically raw, it tastes and feels cooked. Best of all, you can prep this the night before the trip: Squeeze the limes and lemons into one zip-seal bag, and put the chopped ingredients into another zip-seal. All you'll need to do then is catch the fish.

SERVES 4

1 lb (500 g) saltwater fish fillets, rinsed well

1 tablespoon salt

½ cup (4 fl oz/125 ml) freshly squeezed lime juice (from about 6 limes)

½ cup (4 fl oz/125 ml) freshly squeezed lemon juice

1 tablespoon olive oil

1 onion, finely chopped

¼ cup (⅓ oz/10 g) finely chopped cilantro

1 jalapeño or habanero chile, minced (optional)

Tortilla chips, popcorn, Corn Nuts, or similar, for serving

Cut the fish into bite-size chunks and place in a medium bowl. Salt it, then gently turn the fish pieces to ensure even seasoning, and add the lime and lemon juices along with the olive oil. Marinate the fish—covered and either refrigerated or over ice—for at least an hour, or up to 3 or 4 hours. (The longer the marinating, the firmer and more "cooked" the fish will be.) Turn the fish occasionally, or shake the container once in a while, to make sure the marinade is covering all of the fish.

When almost ready to serve, take the fish out of the refrigerator. Add the remaining ingredients and stir gently. Let sit for at least 15 minutes for the flavors to meld. Serve with tortilla chips, popcorn, Corn Nuts, or whatever else is on board.

COCKTAILS FOR YOUR CATCH

Complete the tropical experience with an icy rum drink. Rum drinks run the gamut from sickly sweet to rough and bitter, but our favorites are the ones adopted throughout history by British sailors (who received a daily ration back when they were the rulers of the seas).

DARK 'N' STORMY One simple but worthy classic is the Dark 'n' Stormy, which the sailors stationed in Bermuda concocted in the nineteenth century. Add 2 oz (60 ml) Gosling's Black Seal rum to an ice-filled glass, and top with ginger beer and a generous squeeze of lime. Repeat as desired.

GROG Combine 2 parts water, 1 part rum, lime juice to taste, and dark cane sugar to taste.

RUM PUNCH Blend 2 oz (60 ml) rum with equal parts orange and pineapple juices, plus the juice of ½ lime and a splash of grenadine. Serve with a wedge of pineapple.

RUM FIZZ In a cocktail shaker filled with ice, mix 2 oz (60 ml) rum with equal parts pineapple juice and lemonade. Add a dash of bitters, shake well, and strain into an ice-filled Collins glass. Grate nutmeg on top and serve.

DAIQUIRI A good, honest daiquiri is simple to make and nothing like the fruit slushies found on Bourbon Street. In an ice-filled shaker, add 2 oz (60 ml) light rum, 1 oz (30 ml) fresh lime juice, and 1 teaspoon of superfine sugar. Shake well and strain into a chilled cocktail glass. Garnish with lime.

OPEN FIRE COOKING

Few elements of the outdoors are so naturally and satisfyingly paired together as fire and meat. They work in tandem, they sustain and nourish you, and few meals are more gratifying and enjoyable than the ones made from meat you killed and cooked over a fire you built. Get your tinder ready and some meat prepped: Here are some of the most delicious ways to cook game over flame.

RABBIT ON A STICK

The inconsistent diameter of a rabbit on a skewer makes it easy to turn the loins into asphalt while trying to get the legs cooked. The trick is to stuff the rabbit with a mixture of moist fruit (in this recipe, figs, but feel free to substitute something more your speed) that pairs well with the mild white meat, and wrap it with bacon to keep it from drying out. Also, forget about rotating the horizontal skewer with a constant motion. Instead, use this ingenious trick to lock the rotisserie in place for minutes at a time.

1 First, stir together a dozen fresh figs, a teaspoon of dried thyme, and 2 tablespoons of olive oil (try one flavored with wild mushroom and sage).

2 Stuff the body cavity with the fig-and-herb mixture, then secure it with 3–4 wraps of kitchen twine.

3 Wrap the rabbit in bacon and truss it with more twine to keep the bacon in place. Trussing is easy. Tie a loop around one end of the rabbit with a simple double knot. Stretch 1½ inches (4 cm) of twine along the body, hold it in place with your thumb, wrap the twine around the rabbit, pass it under the first loop, and continue. At the end of the rabbit, pass the twine behind the backstrap, threading it under the wraps. Tie off to the first.

4 Now run the skewer through the rear cavity along the inside of the backbone and out through the neck.

5 Make a rotisserie of two forked sticks on opposite sides of a fire or a stack of hot briquettes, and place the skewer in the forks.

6 Roast the rabbit for about 10 minutes, rotate 180 degrees, then lock the skewer in place with shoelace bows of kitchen twine tied tightly around the forked sticks. Cook for another 10 minutes. Next, rotate 90 degrees and cook for 7–8 minutes, then rotate 180 degrees and cook for another 7–8 minutes.

7 The rabbit is ready when a kitchen thermometer inserted into the fat part of the hind leg reaches 160°F (70°C), or when you just can't resist the smell of bacon, figs, and rabbit any longer. —T.E.N.

FISH ON A LOG

Freshly caught local trout and panfish are small and thin enough to cook quickly, white enough to soak in the flavors of smoke, and fatty enough to stay moist in the heat of an open flame. Best of all, you don't even need a carefully milled and squared plank of wood.

1 Halve an 18- to 24-inch (46- to 62-cm) long, 8- to 12-inch (20- to 30-cm) diameter log. (Cedar is a good choice; stay away from pine, as its resin is too pungent.)

2 Whittle a dozen or so 2-inch (5-cm) wooden pegs, making one end of each sharp.

3 Lightly oil the flat surface of the log round and lay out the fillets or whole fish (scaled and gutted), skin side down. Large fish should be planked vertically. With the point of a knife, poke through the fish to mark the log where the pegs should be, remove the fish, then drill starter holes for the pegs. Replace the fish and tap the pegs into place.

4 Season your catch with salt, pepper, and butter, a spice rub, or insert ginger slivers and sprinkle with teriyaki sauce.

5 Build a tepee fire so the flames will rise at least to the level of the fish.

6 Position the log round beside the fire, 8–18 inches away (depending on the thickness of the fish), using rocks for support. Roll out a strip of aluminum foil in front of the log to reflect heat and aid cooking, but also to catch pieces of fish that might slip off the pegs—where you can snatch them up for a quick snack. Cooking time: 10–15 minutes, or until the meat flakes. —T.E.N.

VENISON STEAKS ON A ROCK

Before there were porcelain-coated grill grates, ceramic infrared bottom burners, and electronic ignition, there were smoking-hot rocks with hunks of wild game on them. Cooking medallions of venison backstrap on hot slabs of once-molten earth is still an outstanding way to enjoy a Cro-Magnon delicacy without ignoring your postmodern foodie affectations.

1 Start by building a good, hot fire to produce a deep bed of coals.

2 While the wood is cooking, find a flat rock that's less than 2 inches (5 cm) thick. Avoid delicate shales and sandstones, and stay away from stream rocks; saturated rocks can explode in a fire. Wash the rock surface and place it at the edge of the coals for 15 minutes to preheat; heating it gradually will lessen the chances of its cracking and splitting. Scoop out the center of the coals to make a shallow bed, and nestle the rock into the coals.

3 Slice your backstrap into ½-inch to ¾-inch (1- to 2-cm) medallions. If you slice them evenly, they will cook at the same rate. Pat the meat dry before heating to guarantee a good sear.

4 Once the rock is hot enough that a drop of water sizzles and vaporizes, brush on a film of flavored olive oil, such as chipotle, then add backstrap medallions and ¼-inch-thick slices of onion. Season with cracked black pepper. Cook the venison and onions 2–3 minutes. Using tongs, remove them to a plate.

5 Turn the rock over, brush away the ashes, and drizzle with more flavored olive oil. Place the medallions and onions on the fresh, hot surface, cooked side up, and top each medallion with an oil-packed sun-dried tomato. Cook for another 2 minutes. Stack an onion slice on top of the meat and sun-dried tomato, and dig in. —T.E.N.

GRILLED DOVE PIZZA

Here's how to cap off an adventurous day afield. With its crispy, smoky crust, grilled pizza is a majestic thing, and this recipe cranks up that majesty by topping the pizza with an earthy combination of dove breasts, wild mushrooms, and sage. Your local pizzeria will usually sell you a round of raw dough, or use fresh or frozen store-bought dough to make life easier.

SERVES 4

3 tablespoons all-purpose flour

1 round uncooked pizza dough

9 tablespoons (5 fl oz/140 ml) olive oil

1 lb (500 g) wild mushrooms (shiitakes work great), stemmed

Salt and freshly ground black pepper

4 dove (or other gamebird) breasts

2 slices bacon

1½ cups (6 oz/185 g) grated Fontina cheese

6–8 fresh sage leaves, chopped

Put 4 toothpicks in water to soak for 30 minutes. Sprinkle the flour on a large cutting board or clean countertop and dust your hands with it, too. Divide the pizza dough in half. (Two smaller pizzas work better on the grill than one large one.) Flatten each half into a disk ¼ inch (6 mm) thick, either stretching by hand or by using a rolling pin. Slather all sides with about 4 tablespoons (2 fl oz/60 ml) of the olive oil, or 1 tablespoon per side, to keep the dough from sticking. Set aside.

Set up your grill for two-level cooking, with one side high (400°F/200°C) and the other medium (350°F/180°C) so you can slide the pizza around and prevent scorching. (For charcoal grills, this means arranging the coals so one side has a large pile and the other side has a smaller pile).

While the grill is heating, put the mushroom caps in a bowl, add 3 tablespoons of the oil, and gently toss to coat. Set aside. Salt and pepper the dove breasts and wrap each with a half slice of bacon, securing the bacon with the soaked toothpicks. Put the cheese in a bowl.

When the grill is ready, arrange all your ingredients close at hand. Grill the dove breasts over medium heat, turning once, until the bacon is cooked. Arrange the mushrooms on the same medium side of the grill, and cook, turning once, until tender, about 6 minutes total.

Remove the toothpicks and chop the dove breasts—bacon and all—into small pieces. Put these pieces in a bowl. Slice the grilled mushrooms and add these to the bowl, then add the chopped sage.

Drape the dough rounds onto the hot side of the grill. Within a minute or so, they will begin to puff up. Using tongs and a wide spatula (or a pizza peel, if you're so equipped), slide the crusts to the medium side and cook until the bottoms are firm and browned, about 4 minutes. Flip the crusts over, back onto the hot side, and cook for 1 more minute.

Slide the crusts to the medium side. Drizzle or brush the tops with the remaining 2 tablespoons olive oil, then divide the cheese between them. Do likewise with the dove and mushroom mixture. Cover to melt the cheese, and cook 3–5 more minutes. (It's okay if the bottom is a little scorched.) Transfer to a platter, sprinkle with salt and pepper, and serve.

Cleaning your grates—and keeping them clean—is the best way to keep food from sticking to them. After the grates cool, toss them upside down on the grass and leave them overnight. The dew and various lawn enzymes will loosen any crusted debris; a squirt from the hose banishes the rest.

If it's too late to employ this method and you're faced with a cruddy, sticky grill and a fish to cook, don't despair. Preheat the grill with the grates in place, and when the top grates are hot, use a wire brush (or balled-up tinfoil held with tongs) to scrub them clean.

Another good practice is to oil the top grate just prior to grilling, again to prevent sticking. Drizzle oil onto a paper towel. (Hint: Use an oil with a high smoke point that tolerates heat, like safflower, peanut, or canola—not your prize extra-virgin olive oil.) Using tongs, rub the oil-soaked towel across the hot grates right before cooking. For good measure, oil your food as well.

One last tip: If you're unsure when your grill is hot enough to start cooking, hold your hand three inches over the grate and start counting. If you can't make it to three "Mississippi"s before it's so hot that you have to pull your hand away, your fire is ready.

PERFECTLY GRILLED WHOLE FISH

The perfect way for an angler who loves to cook to show off his fish is serving it whole, fresh off the grill, with crispy skin and moist flesh. Problem is, that's not usually how it happens. Here's how to grill a whole fish so it's juicy, smoky, and beautifully intact. Snapper, bass, trout, flounder, striped bass, and bluefish work best.

SERVES 2–4

1 whole fish, up to around 2 lb (1 kg) or so, scaled and gutted

1 tablespoon vegetable oil

Salt and freshly ground black pepper

1 lemon

Start a hot fire in your grill. Once the grates are hot, turn down to medium (350°F/180°C), or, if using charcoal, simply rake the coals to ensure an even layer of heat. Clean and oil the grill grate (*see left*).

Make 3 diagonal cuts in each side of the fish, straight to the bone. Rub both sides of the fish with the oil, then salt and pepper it.

Lay the fish on the grill, uncovered, and go away—grab a beer, check the score of the game, anything. After 5 minutes, use tongs to gently pry the fish from the grates, easing it free from any sticky spots. Set it back down on the same side and go away for another 2–3 minutes.

Slide a long-handled spatula beneath the fish's heaviest section and gently roll it over. Pretend that it's a baby on a rug who's fallen asleep on your remote. To get that remote, you want to roll that baby up and over without waking him.

Continue cooking for up to 10 minutes, depending on the size of the fish. To check for doneness, use a knife to probe the diagonal cuts you made in the flesh. The meat should look opaque. Gently transfer the fish to a platter, squeeze some lemon juice onto it, and serve.

DOVES FROM HELL

Lock up the children. Have lots of cold beer on hand—and maybe an EMT. These habanero-slathered dove breasts, inspired by the tear-inducing chicken wings at the East Coast Grill in Cambridge, Massachusetts, are to the familiar bacon-and-jalapeño prepared doves what a grenade launcher is to a .30-.30. Seriously: They're hot. You've been warned.

SERVES 4

CHILE-MUSTARD SAUCE

⅓ cup (3 fl oz/80 ml) prepared yellow mustard

2–8 habanero chiles, seeded and chopped

2 tablespoons minced ginger

1 tablespoon minced garlic

2 scallions (both green and white sections), finely chopped

Pinch of allspice

1 tablespoon curry powder

1 tablespoon ground cumin

1 tablespoon ground coriander

2 tablespoons dried oregano

3 tablespoons freshly cracked black pepper

2 tablespoons kosher salt

DOVES

1 lb (500 g) dove breasts (about 15 or so mourning doves)

1 lime, halved

2 tablespoons freshly chopped cilantro

MAKE THE CHILE-MUSTARD SAUCE Combine all the sauce ingredients in a blender and purée until smooth.

MAKE THE DOVES Start a medium-hot fire (375°F/190°C) in your grill.

Pour the sauce over the dove breasts in a bowl, turning them to coast evenly.

Grill the breasts directly over the flame, turning occasionally, until well browned, about 4 minutes per side. To check for doneness, cut into one piece to see that the meat is medium-rare. Or use a meat thermometer—125°F (52°C) is ideal. Let the breasts rest for a few minutes after cooking.

▶ **SERVING TIP** Place the grilled breasts in a bowl, squeeze the lime halves over them, and toss them with the cilantro. Serve with jalapeño Cheddar cornbread (at right).

WILD SIDE: JALAPEÑO CHEDDAR CORNBREAD

Bacon drippings

1 cup (5 oz/155 g) flour

1 cup (7 oz/220 g) cornmeal

1 cup (8 fl oz/250 ml) buttermilk

⅓ cup (3 fl oz/80 ml) canola oil

2 tablespoons sugar

2 teaspoons baking powder

½ teaspoon salt

1 egg

⅓ cup (1½ oz/45 g) shredded Cheddar cheese

¼ cup (2 oz/60 g) seeded and diced jalapeño chiles (about 6 medium)

Prepare this spicy side for a twist on classic comfort food. It pairs nicely with the heat of the doves, and it's good on its own, to boot. Preheat the oven to 400°F (200°C). Grease a 10-inch (25-cm) cast-iron pan with bacon drippings. Combine all the ingredients except the Cheddar and jalapeños in a medium bowl, and beat together. Fold in the Cheddar and jalapeños until well combined, and pour into the prepared pan.

Place in the oven and bake for 15 minutes. Check for doneness by inserting a toothpick into the center of the cornbread. If it comes out clean, it's ready. If not, bake for a few more minutes, but no longer than 20 minutes total. Serve warm.

SERVES 6–8

WILD CHEF PROJECT: THE WILLOW SKILLET

In 60 minutes you can build a fire, clean your catch, weave a grill, and burn the dishes. Oh yeah, and eat the freshest fish you've ever tasted. These instructions are for a couple of eating-size fish for two people. But there's no limit to how big a grill you can weave from branches, so supersize this model for larger fish or cuts of game.

1 From a pliable willow sapling, cut the following pieces: a Y-stick with a foot-long (30-cm) stub and forks 3 feet (1 m) long; two 20-inch (50-cm) branches; and six 14-inch (35-cm) branches. Snip off all twigs and soak in warm water.

2 Twist the fork branches into the shape of a racket. Start at the thick ends and move toward the tips, working them back and forth a bit at a time, being careful not to split the wood.

3 Lay a 20-inch (50-cm) branch across the center of the racket, then weave in the other 20-inch (50-cm) branch so they cross in the middle. Pre-bend the others so that they can be woven in with enough tension to stay firmly in place.

▶ **SERVING TIP:** To help infuse your catch with flavor, top the fish with onions, lemon, and bacon. Or just scarf it down plain.

FOUR TRAIL MIX RECIPES

Trail mix is an everpresent camping classic, suited for hikes, hunts, and those long hours between meals. A little salt, a little sweet, something crunchy and chewy and altogether hearty and satisfying. You could pay $8.99 a pound for prefabricated trail mix from the grocery store or local co-op. Or you could keep your self-respect intact and mix your own from a pick-and-choose assortment tailored to your design. Just be sure to make enough for everyone, and don't skimp on your favorite ingredient.

THE CLASSIC Raisins, peanuts, M&M's, and granola.

THE TROPICAL Smoked almonds, butterscotch chips, dried banana chips, dried pineapple chunks, and flaked coconut.

THE PORTLANDIA Wheat germ, dark chocolate–covered coffee beans, macadamia nuts, chopped dried figs, and salted or unsalted sunflower seeds.

THE INNER CHILD Rice Chex, Cheerios, pretzel sticks, plain M&M's, and salted peanuts. Mix together, pour melted white chocolate over all, spread onto wax paper to cool, and break into clumps. —T.E.N.

TRUCKER'S RICE WITH VENISON JERKY

Years ago, on a fishing trip in Brazil, the camp cook served me a fragrant bowl of meat and rice. "We call this *arroz de carreteiro*," the cook said, translating that as "trucker's rice." The meat was dried beef, or jerky, which, cooked with rice, made for a simple meal for long-haul truckers to prepare when traversing Brazil's wide open spaces, where fresh ingredients can be hard to come by. Easy and addictive, it has since become one of my camping staples.

SERVES 6

8 oz (250 g) venison (or beef) jerky

3 tablespoons vegetable oil

1 yellow onion, finely chopped

2 cloves garlic, chopped

1 tomato, peeled and chopped

Freshly ground black pepper

2 cups (14 oz/440 g) long-grain rice

1 bay leaf

3 tablespoons chopped Italian parsley

Salt (optional)

Salsa or hot sauce for serving (optional)

Cover the jerky entirely with water and soak for several hours—1 hour, at the very least—to rehydrate. Changing the water once or twice will help reduce the saltiness.

Remove the jerky from the water, then dice into fine cubes. Heat the oil in a medium-size pot or Dutch oven over medium heat, then add the onion. Sauté, stirring frequently, until the onion is translucent and limp, about 5 minutes. Add the garlic and cook for 1 minute, stirring, then add the drained jerky and tomato, raise the heat to high, and continue to cook, stirring, for about another minute. Add some pepper. Add the rice and bay leaf, and stir to coat the rice with the oil, then add 4½ cups (36 fl oz/1.1 l) water and bring to a boil. Reduce the heat to low, cover, and cook until nearly all the water is absorbed, about 16 minutes. Turn off the heat and let sit for about 5 minutes.

When the rice is ready, gently stir in the parsley. Taste for salt; the jerky should provide enough saltiness, but add more if desired. Serve with salsa or hot sauce on the side.

FRIED CRAPPIE

You pray for those days when the crappie fishing is so relentlessly good that you're giggling like a kid and the only things you're lacking in life are another stringer and an extra hour on the water. But what do you do with that pile of freshly caught crappies spilling out of your cooler? Call your pals for a mega-fry. You'll want some help filleting, dredging, and battering the fish, and providing side dishes. (You'd be surprised what people will do for fried fish and free beer.)

SERVES EVERYONE YOU KNOW

12 fl oz (375 ml) ale or any full-bodied beer

1½ cups (8¼ oz/255 g) corn flour

1 teaspoon salt

1 teaspoon paprika

½ teaspoon cayenne pepper

2 tablespoons minced Italian parsley

Fresh peanut, canola, safflower, or corn oil for deep-frying

1 lb (500 g) crappie fillets, cut into fingerlike strips

1 cup (5 oz/155 g) all-purpose flour

Salsa, lemon wedges, tartar sauce, and hot sauce for serving

Empty the beer into a large bowl. (It hurts, I know.) Add the corn flour, salt, paprika, cayenne, and parsley to the bowl, and whisk until you have a light and frothy batter. Refrigerate for at least 1 hour or up to 5 days.

In a deep fryer or deep skillet, heat at least 2 inches (5 cm) of oil to 375°F (190°C) on a candy thermometer. Dredge the fillets in the flour, shaking off any excess, then dip them in the beer batter, coating them well. Fry them in the oil until perfectly golden—remove the pieces as soon as they float to the top of the oil. Drain on paper towels.

Serve in shifts, so that your guests are getting their fish hot from the fryer, accompanied with the salsa, lemon wedges, tartar sauce, and hot sauce.

If possible, make this an outside operation—the odor will take weeks to air out of a kitchen.

And don't forget to "test" the fish as it comes out of the oil (the beer will need regular sampling, too).

EAT MORE BASS

"I love bass," says Ray Scott. "I love it." Taken out of context, this statement hardly comes as a surprise. By founding the Bass Anglers Sportsmen Society (B.A.S.S.) in 1967, and introducing bassers to the concept of catch-and-release fishing several years later, Scott has done more than any other man alive to promote and perpetuate the largemouth bass. If bass fishing is a religion—and it can seem like one, with its rules and rituals and moments of rod-bending rapture—then Scott is that religion's sacred prophet, its original dispenser of commandments up to and including "thou shalt not kill your catch." Which is why Scott's statement, folded back into context, might startle some of the faithful: Ray Scott is talking here about his love for eating bass. "It'll probably shock a lot of people to hear me say this," he admits. "Well, I'm sorry, but we're not going to hell for filleting a bass."

Already I can hear the grumbling, and I don't mean the stomach kind. Bass anglers tend to be the least-hungry fishermen on the water, releasing their catches with rigid, almost fundamentalist discipline. And that's generally a good thing. "I'd rather hear a 40-year-old man say he'd never eaten a bass in his life than have everyone taking their bass home to the table," Scott says. But in certain fisheries—farm ponds, especially—regular harvesting benefits the fishing. "If your objective is to grow quality bass," he says, "you do that by removing some of the competition." Still, many bassers just can't stomach—pardon the pun—the idea of watching their beloved quarry sizzling in a pan. As one angler once told Texas fisheries biologist Bob Lusk: "Eating a bass is like eating the family dog."

Maybe so. But contrary to widespread perception, they can be downright delicious. Largemouth bass has never enjoyed a sterling culinary reputation, which is partly why Scott's campaign to get bass anglers to lay aside their stringers succeeded so well. The allegation is that bass sometimes tastes weedy or grassy, a semi-accurate charge that requires some qualification. As with any fish or animal, the flavor of a bass's flesh hinges on its environment—in this case, the water it swims in and the diet it survives on. A largemouth taken from a hot, shallow, mucky, overgrown, and swampily-aromatic pond will taste, well, the way you might expect it would; as a court bouillon flavors the fish that's cooking in it, so too does a body of water flavor the fish that inhabit it. The same applies with a bass's diet: Florida largemouths that have been dining on freshwater shrimp are said to have a startlingly sweet flavor, quite different from that of farm-pond largemouths that have been grazing on midsummer grasshoppers.

Dwelling on the occasional off-flavors, however, obscures one very tasty point: The flesh of freshwater basses is white, flaky, and low in oil, with a mild, faintly-sweet taste that lends itself to a wide range of flavor adornments. More succinctly, as Scott says, it's "awful good." Sacrilege? Perhaps. As a gamefish, the bass has a kind of brawny, blue-collar grandeur to it, a muscularity and bellicosity that's endeared it to millions of fishermen; only a fraction of those anglers, however, knows the delicate flip side to the bass that only a fork can make apparent. One's love for bass, as Scott shows, can extend beyond the boat all the way into the kitchen.

PAN-ROASTED LARGEMOUTH BASS WRAPPED IN COUNTRY HAM

The largemouth bass inhabits every state in the continental United States, but I've always considered it, at heart, a Southern fish. This may be owing to the Mississippi roots of my own bass fishing, or, more likely, to a general angling precept that says the farther south you go, the better the bassing—and the more devoted the bass fishermen. In this recipe, I've thrown together about as much of the Deep South as I can fit on a plate, including a barbecue vinaigrette based on a creation by John Fleer, the former chef at the Inn at Blackberry Farm in Walland, Tennessee. If you don't have local access to bona fide country hams, substitute prosciutto. An un-oaked chardonnay would pair well with this dish, but you could also deepen its drawl that much further by serving it with a first-rate bourbon.

VINAIGRETTE
1 teaspoon molasses

¼ cup (2 fl oz/60 ml) brewed coffee

½ cup (4 fl oz/125 ml) beef stock

¼ cup (2 fl oz/60 ml) plus ½ cup (4 fl oz/125 ml) balsamic vinegar

2 teaspoons Worcestershire sauce

1 teaspoon plus 1 tablespoon Tabasco or other hot sauce

1 cup (8 fl oz/250 ml)

Salt and freshly ground black pepper

GRITS
2 cups (14 oz/440 g) uncooked grits

4 tablespoons butter

2 tablespoons heavy cream

1 tablespoon Tabasco or other hot sauce

FISH
1 tablespoon olive oil

4 thin slices country ham

1 egg white, lightly beaten

4 largemouth bass fillets, skin and lateral line removed

MAKE THE VINAIGRETTE In a small saucepan, combine the molasses, coffee, beef stock, and ¼ cup (2 fl oz/60 ml) of the balsamic vinegar. Cook over medium-high heat until reduced by half. In a medium bowl, combine this mixture with the remaining ½ cup (4 fl oz/125 ml) balsamic vinegar, the Worcestershire sauce, and 1 teaspoon Tabasco sauce. Gradually whisk in 1 cup olive oil. Salt and pepper to taste, and set aside.

MAKE THE GRITS Cook the grits according to the package directions. Then stir in the butter, cream, and 1 tablespoon Tabasco sauce. Salt and pepper to taste, and keep warm.

MAKE THE FISH Preheat the oven to 350°F (175°C). Brush the ham slices with the egg white and wrap around the fillets. If the slices are wider than the fillets, trim them so that the ends of the fish are poking out. Seal the seams of the ham slices with more egg white if necessary.

In an oven-safe skillet, heat 1 tablespoon olive oil over medium-high heat until shimmery but not smoking. Add the ham-wrapped fillets and sear on all sides, about 30 seconds per side. Transfer the skillet to the oven for about 5 minutes, or until the fish is opaque.

To serve, spoon ½ cup (3.5 oz/110 g) or so of grits on the center of a plate. Top with a ham-wrapped fillet, and spoon the vinaigrette over the fish and grits.

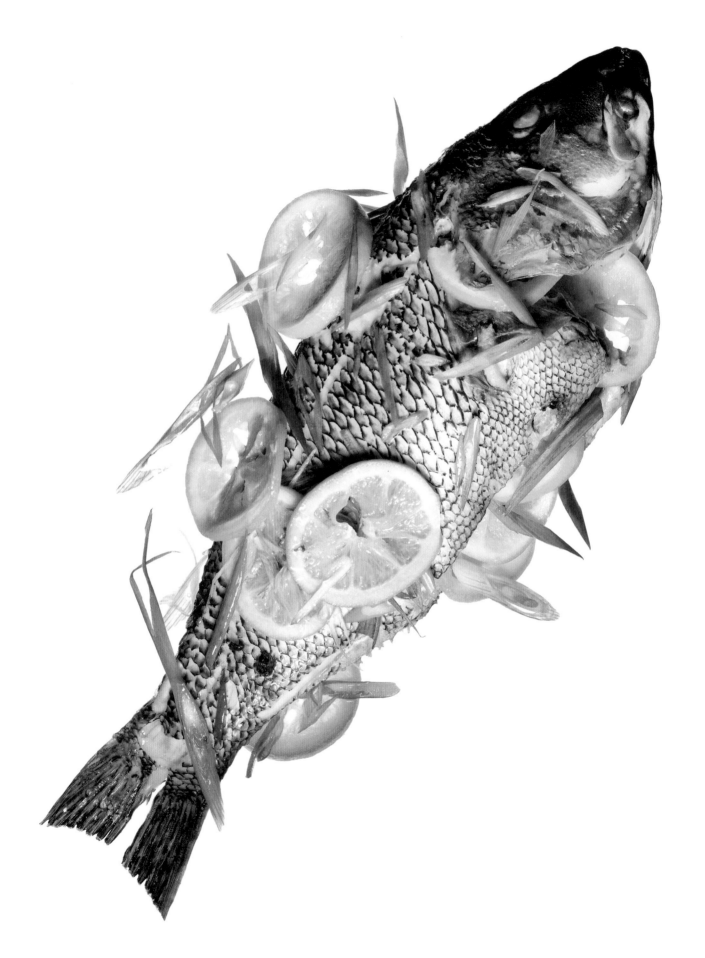

WOK-STEAMED WHOLE FISH

This dish, a riff on an ancient Chinese method for cooking fish in which the flavor of steamed whole fish is turbocharged by a drizzling of smoking-hot oil, is great at home, but even better at camp or the beach. All you need, besides a campfire, is a wok with a lid, a heatproof plate, an oven mitt, and a few packable garnishes. Any whole fish will do, so long as it'll fit inside the wok.

SERVES 6

2 lemons*

½ tablespoon kosher salt

1 tablespoon sugar

1 whole fish (black sea bass, largemouth), gutted and scaled

2 tablespoons peanut or vegetable oil

1 bunch green onions, trimmed and sliced

*Supermarket lemons are often waxed. To remove the wax, blanch them in boiling water for 30 seconds, then wipe them with a towel.

Preserve the lemons using this quick-preserve method: Slice the lemons, discard any seeds, and toss them (along with their juices) with the salt and the sugar in a lidded jar. Let the lemons sit at room temperature for 3 hours, occasionally giving the jar a good shake. Refrigerate until ready to use. (The lemons will last up to a week in the fridge.) Put the fish on a heatproof plate and insert several slices of the lemon in the body cavity.

Place a wok over high heat. (If you're doing this on a campfire, just place the wok in the hottest part of the fire.) To make a steaming platform, form a grid in the wok with 4 chopsticks or other sticks, or build a platform out of crumpled-up aluminum foil; the idea is to elevate the plate to keep it above the water. Add enough water (seawater is fine) to almost touch the platform. When the water boils, carefully lower the plate onto the platform and cover the wok. Steam the fish 6–10 minutes, depending on size and thickness. (Check after 6 minutes by poking the fish with a knife; it will flake easily when done.)

Remove the plate from the wok and set aside, using the wok cover to keep it warm. Empty the wok, then return it to the heat. When the wok is hot and dry, add the oil. As the oil is heating, sprinkle the scallions over the fish. Top the fish with a few preserved lemon slices.

Now the fun part. When the oil is smoking (you want it to be dangerously hot), drizzle it onto the fish and enjoy the wild crackling. Serve the fish immediately after the hot-oil drizzling demonstration.

WILD CHEF PROJECT: THE ULTIMATE SUMMER GIG

Frog gigging is buggy, mucky, messy, and about as highbrow as picking your toes in public. In short, it's perfect summer fun for boys of any age. It's caveman simple, but there are a few tricks you should know. For starters, don't go too early in summer—give those bullfrogs a chance to lay on the meat. And don't wait too long—gigging a gigged-out pond is like batting cleanup in a game of spin the bottle. Maybe you'd just better get on with it and go this weekend. And if your buddies tell you to grow up, just tell them you will . . . when summer is over.

MAKE A WICKED FROG FORK

Frog gigging feeds the stomach and the soul, because there's something downright spiritual about a lily-fringed frog pond on a new-moon night. You can use a retro cane pole—or you can get fancy with this telescoping gig fashioned from a 16-foot (5 m) bream pole. It's perfect for any small-boat frogman or somebody who needs a pole that will fit in a car.

1 Remove the butt cap, then slide out the rod-tip end of the nested sections. Saw off the front end of the pole at the point where it snugly fits inside the gig head.

2 Drill a 1/8-inch (3-mm) hole through the gig shaft and pole. Remove the gig head and coat the inside with epoxy, then affix the gig head using a #6-32 stainless-steel bolt, washer, and locking nut. Let the glue set, and you're done.

3 To clean your frogs, remove the legs above the hips. A perfect cut keeps the legs attached. Pull the skin down to the ankle and cut off the feet. Dredge legs through a milk-and-egg bath, then batter. Fry in peanut oil. —T.E.N.

COOK YOUR CATCH IN A REFLECTOR OVEN

Another camp tool handy to have around is a reflector oven, which cooks by directing a campfire's heat down toward a cooking shelf that holds the food. You can buy a traditional reflector oven and use it time after time, or you can make your own from aluminum foil.

First, cut two branched sticks about 20 inches (50 cm) below the Y. Drive them into the ground at the edge of the fire ring, 18 inches (45 cm) apart. Wrap a 22-inch (55-cm)-long stick with heavy-duty aluminum foil, place it in the forks of the Y-sticks, and unroll foil at a 45-degree angle away from the fire to the ground. Anchor the foil with another stick and unroll a shelf of foil toward the fire, then tear off. Place four dry rocks on the bottom of the shelf. These will hold the baking rack or pan.

To create the oven sides, wrap one of the upright Y-sticks with foil. Unroll the foil around the back of the oven. Tear off the foil. Repeat on the other side. Pinch the two pieces of foil together.

To broil fish, line a baking pan (or simply use the bottom shelf as the baking pan) with onion slices. Add the fillets, seasoned with lemon juice, salt, and pepper. An easy way to punch it up is to slather with store-bought chipotle sauce. Top with a few more onion slices. Flip once, and cook until fish flakes with a fork. —T.E.N.

CEDAR-ROASTED CHAR

When Jeff McInnis—the chef at Yardbird Southern Table & Bar in Miami Beach—isn't cooking, he's likely fishing. In this recipe, the Florida native combines his passions, creating a summertime symphony on the plate. At Yardbird, McInnis uses Arctic char, but any fresh fish will shine here, even a lunker bass.

SERVES 6

CORN SAUCE

Kernels from 15 ears of fresh corn

½ cup (4 fl oz/125 ml) champagne (nothing too pricey)

6 tablespoons (3 oz/90 g) unsalted butter, cut into pieces

Salt and freshly ground black pepper

SUCCOTASH

1 cup (5 oz/155 g) diced carrots

3 ears corn on the cob

2 cups (14 oz/440 g) baby lima beans

¼ cup (2 fl oz/60 ml) plus 2 tablespoons olive oil

1 cup (3 oz/90 g) thinly sliced leeks, white part only

Bouquet garni of 3 thyme sprigs and 1 bay leaf, tied together with kitchen twine

1 large tomato, seeded and diced small

6 Arctic char, salmon, or other fish fillets, about 5 oz (155 g) each

MAKE THE CORN SAUCE Put the corn kernels in a blender and purée for about a minute until very smooth. Set a fine-mesh sieve over a bowl and pour in the purée to strain. Press on the pulp to extract as much juice as possible. Discard the pulp. Combine this corn juice and the champagne in a small saucepan over medium-high heat. Cook, stirring constantly, for about 3 minutes, or until it thickens almost to the consistency of pudding. (The sauce at the bottom may appear slightly scorched; keep stirring, and things will be okay.) Reduce the heat to low and stir in the butter one piece at a time, to form a silky sauce. Remove from the heat; the natural cornstarch will thicken it. Season with salt and pepper and set aside.

MAKE THE SUCCOTASH Bring a large pot of water to a boil over high heat. Add the carrots and cook for about 3 minutes, or until tender. Remove with a slotted spoon and transfer to a bowl of ice water. Add the ears of corn, and remove when the water returns to a boil, in about 3 minutes. Set the corn aside and add the lima beans to the same water. Reduce the heat to low and simmer for 10 minutes, or until tender. Drain, and set the lima beans aside. Cut the kernels off the corncobs and discard the cobs.

Heat ¼ cup (2 fl oz/60 ml) of the olive oil in a large, shallow saucepan over medium-high heat. Add the leeks and sauté for a few minutes. Add the *bouquet garni* to the pan. Add the reserved carrots, lima beans, and corn along with the tomato, and season generously with salt and pepper. Cook for about 2 minutes, or until just warmed through; remove the herbs, cover, and remove from the heat.

Now you're ready to cook the fish. Preheat the oven to 425°F (220°C). Lightly oil the fillets with the remaining 2 tablespoons olive oil, and season with salt and pepper. Place the fish on a thin cedar plank and bake 7–9 minutes, depending on its thickness.

▶ **SERVING TIP** Spoon a generous portion of succotash onto the plates, top with the fish, brush each fillet with the sauce, and torch before serving—using a kitchen torch, lightly brown the sauce-brushed fish, as you would a crème brûlée. Alternatively, brush the fillets with corn sauce while they're still on the plank and place them under a broiler, very close to the heat. Remove when the sauce has browned and serve at once.

WHOLE FRIED CATFISH WITH GREEN ONIONS & "DICKEY SAUCE"

This recipe is the real deal—deep-fried catfish as it's served at Taylor Grocery in Oxford, Mississippi. "Dickey sauce" is tartar sauce, renamed by locals in memory of the late poet and novelist James Dickey (*Deliverance*). When small bowls of tartar sauce were brought to the table, Dickey—famed for his formidable whiskey consumption—grabbed a spoon and gulped down all the sauce in his bowl. "That," he announced, "was the best soup I've ever eaten."

SERVES 4

DICKEY SAUCE

¾ cup (6 fl oz/180 ml) Miracle Whip

½ cup (4 fl oz/125 ml) mayonnaise

¼ cup (1½ oz/45 g) relish

¼ cup (1½ oz/45 g) finely chopped yellow onion

3 tablespoons fresh lemon juice

BATTER

2 eggs

Dash of Worcestershire sauce

Dash of hot sauce

2½ cups (20 fl oz/625 ml) milk

1 cup (7 oz/220 g) yellow cornmeal

⅓ cup (2 oz/60 g) all-purpose flour

1 teaspoon lemon pepper

Salt and freshly ground pepper

4 wild catfish, skinned and beheaded (about 1½ lb/750 g each)

2 qt (64 fl oz/2 l) peanut oil

8 green onions

MAKE THE DICKEY SAUCE In a medium bowl, fold together the Miracle Whip, mayonnaise, relish, onion, and lemon juice. Cover and refrigerate until ready to use.

MAKE THE BATTER Combine the eggs, Worcestershire, hot sauce, and milk together in a large bowl and beat until frothy. In a shallow dish large enough to contain the fish, whisk together the cornmeal, flour, lemon pepper, and salt and black pepper to taste.

With a small knife, deeply score both sides of the catfish 4 times across, about 1½ inches (4 cm) apart. Dip the catfish into the egg wash, then dredge it completely with the cornmeal mixture, evenly coating the fish; set it aside.

In a large pot or deep fryer, heat the oil to 325°F (165°C). Add the fish—one at a time—and cook until golden brown and crisp, 7–8 minutes. Remove and place on paper towels to drain.

Serve garnished with green onions and accompanied with Dickey sauce.

BUTTER-BRAISED FISH

Technically, fish can last up to half a year in a freezer, but their quality starts to slide after the first month. Braising those longer-term residents of your deep freeze in butter, however, provides the ideal rescue: It moistens and flavors the fish to luxurious extremes, yielding forkfuls that melt in your mouth. A note of caution: This is rich, so if anyone at your table is sporting a pacemaker, you might want to sound a warning, or serve with a side of Lipitor.

SERVES 4

1 cup (8 fl oz/250 ml) heavy cream

1 lb (4 sticks/500 g) cold butter, cut into pieces, plus 2 tablespoons

4 large leeks, white and pale green parts, thoroughly washed and roughly chopped

4 skinless fish fillets, about 6 oz (185 g) each

Salt and freshly ground black pepper

Preheat the oven to 300°F (150°C). Pour the cream into an ovenproof pot over high heat and add 1 cup (8 fl oz/250 ml) water. When it comes to a boil, turn down the heat to medium and whisk in 1 lb of the butter pieces. Keep the whisk going, and don't let the liquid boil—you want the mixture to emulsify into a saucelike consistency. If it doesn't, mix it in a blender.

Melt the 2 remaining tablespoons of butter in a sauté pan over medium heat. Add the leeks and slowly sauté until meltingly tender, about 12–15 minutes. Set aside.

Season the fillets with salt and pepper. Set the butter mixture over medium heat and bring it to a simmer. Gently add the fish. When it returns to a simmer, cover the pot and place it in the oven. Cook 10–15 minutes until done.

When the fish is done cooking, return the pan with the leeks to the stove over medium-low heat, just to warm them through. Add ¼ cup (2 fl oz/60 ml) of the fish-cooking liquid and season with salt and pepper to taste.

▶ **SERVING TIP** Divide the leeks into four bowls and top with a fillet.

AN EASY (AND EASIER) WAY TO CLEAN LEEKS

You want to find true grit in your hunting companions and partners in crime, but preferably not in your food. Leeks, those vaguely classier distant cousins of the common onion, grow best in sandy soil, and oftentimes this sand gets trapped within the layers as they develop. It's worth always cleaning leeks extra carefully to make sure you're not adding a peck of dirt to your silky braise.

There are two methods to clean a stubborn leek: the easy way, and the easier way. Take your pick.

EASY After trimming away the tough green leaves, split the white and pale green portion of the leek straight down the middle, lengthwise. Rinse under cold running water, separating the layers with your fingers a bit to rinse out any dirt trapped there. Proceed to slice or chop as directed by your chosen recipe.

EASIER After trimming away the tough green leaves, take the white and pale green portion of the leek and slice it thinly crosswise with a sharp knife. Put the rounds into a bowl of cold water and, using your thumb, push the rounds apart into rings and swish them around in the water to wash away any dirt, sand, or other grit. Transfer the rings to a colander, drain, and chop as needed (or leave the rings whole, depending on the recipe).

THE SWEET LIFE

With all the hearty things you can cook up in camp, it might be easy to forget about a sweet treat to cap off your fireside feast. But desserts needn't be an afterthought. Here are five dessert options that are as easy to fix as they are sinfully good.

BLUEBERRY-MUFFIN ORANGES

Pour prepared muffin mix (follow the directions on the box, and substitute applesauce for vegetable oil if you so choose) into half of a hollowed-out orange. Place the other empty half over the top, wrap everything tightly in tinfoil, and bake directly in a bed of hot coals for 10 to 15 minutes. This trick keeps the muffins moist and adds a delicious orange flavor. —D.D.

DEEP-FRIED OREOS

If you're at home, pop about a dozen Oreos into the freezer for 30 minutes or so. If you're at camp, put them in the cooler for at least an hour. You want that filling to get nice and firm so it doesn't all melt away when it hits the hot oil.

While the cookies are chilling, get your oil ready. Pour about 1½ to 2 inches (4 to 5 cm) vegetable or peanut oil into a Dutch oven and set the pot over medium-high heat. Meanwhile, make a batter by blending boxed buttermilk pancake mix with water to a consistency thick enough to stick to the Oreo. When the oil hits 375°F (190°C), dip the cookies into the batter and carefully drop them into the hot oil.

After 15 seconds or so, flip each cookie using a pair of bamboo skewers. Wait another 15 seconds, then pull the Oreos out with a slotted spoon and drain them on paper towels. Before you pop the piping hot nuggets of goo into your mouth, up the buzz factor with a light dusting of powdered sugar. —D.D.

QUESADILLA S'MORES

No campfires allowed? No problem. Place a handful each of chocolate chips, mini marshmallows, and crumbled graham crackers between two flour tortillas. Toast on a hot nonstick griddle, flipping once, until the inside is melted. It's just as good as it sounds. —D.D.

DUTCH OVEN DUMP COBBLER

Dump 3 cans of pie filling, 2 boxed cake mixes, 1 stick sliced butter, and 2 cups of lemon-lime soda (yes, you read that right) into a 12-inch Dutch oven. Bake for 45 minutes to 1 hour. This is one of the easiest camp desserts you'll ever make—and one of the most delicious. —D.D.

SHUTTER UPS

The Shutter Up—a chewy and seriously addictive twist on the most iconic outdoor dessert, the s'more—was born at a summer camp. Its name implies just what the treat did to wound-up campers who wouldn't, well, shut up.

To make them, you'll need marshmallows, some caramel squares, and either chocolate chip cookies or graham crackers. The original Shutter Up left Hershey's out of the picture, but if you can't imagine a s'more—in any form—without some chocolate, be our guest.

Once you've built a fire, slide your marshmallow onto a stick and follow it with a caramel square, so you've got a sweet shish kebob. Roast it over the fire (flip back to page 42 for instructions on how to roast a marshmallow to gooey perfection). When the marshmallow is golden brown, take your cookies or graham crackers and slide off the marshmallow just as if you were making a s'more. Here's where the magic happens: The softened caramel will fold inside the marshmallow and the whole thing will be a warm, heavenly mess of caramel-marshmallow goop.

The Shutter Up is sure to leave you speechless. That is, right up until you ask for seconds. —C.J.L.

INDEX

weldon**owen**

President, CEO Terry Newell
VP, Publisher Roger Shaw
Executive Editor Mariah Bear
Editor Bridget Fitzgerald
Project Editor Sarah P. Clegg
Creative Director Kelly Booth
Art Director William Mack
Project Art Director/Designer Debbie Berne
Designer Michel Gadwa
Illustration and Photography Coordinator Conor Buckley
Production Director Chris Hemesath
Production Manager Michelle Duggan

Weldon Owen would also like to thank Marisa Solís and
Katharine Moore for editorial assistance. Sarah Edelstein
provided design and production help.

© 2013 Weldon Owen Inc.
415 Jackson Street
San Francisco, CA 94111
www.weldonowen.com

All rights reserved, including the right of reproduction in whole
or in part in any form

Field & Stream and Weldon Owen are divisions of **BONNIER**

Library of Congress Control Number on file with the publisher

ISBN 13: 978-1-61628-547-0
ISBN 10: 1-61628-547-8

10 9 8 7 6 5 4 3

2014 2015
Printed in China by 1010 Printing International.

FIELD & STREAM

Executive Vice President Eric Zinczenko
Editor-in-Chief Anthony Licata
Executive Editor Mike Toth
Managing Editor Jean McKenna
Deputy Editors Dave Hurteau, Colin Kearns, Slaton L. White
Copy Chief Donna L. Ng
Senior Editor Joe Cermele
Assistant Editor Kristyn Brady
Design Director Sean Johnston
Photography Director John Toolan
Deputy Art Director Pete Sucheski
Associate Art Directors Kim Gray, James A. Walsh
Production Manager Judith Weber
Digital Director Nate Matthews
Online Content Editor David Maccar
Online Producer Kurt Shulitz
Assistant Online Editor Martin Leung

2 Park Avenue
New York, NY 10016
www.fieldandstream.com

CREDITS

Contributing Editors:
T. Edward Nickens: pages 21, 26, 27, 33, 42, 45, 48, 67, 78, 87, 130,
135, 140, 141, 162, 166, 181, 188, 196, 204
David Draper: pages 23, 104, 107, 117, 122, 143, 151, 152, 157,
159, 166, 175
Colin Kearns: pages 18, 21, 22, 30, 36, 47, 73, 95, 117, 144
Dave Hurteau: pages 27, 78, 96
Will Brantley: pages 33, 208
Hank Shaw: pages 34, 152
Rick Bass: page 35
Phil Bourjaily: page 157
Joe Cermele: page 182
Sarah P. Clegg: page 175
Scott Cookman: page 51
Tom Keer: page 96
CJ Lotz: page 210
Keith McCafferty: page 127
John Merwin: page 140
David E. Petzal: page 26
Steven Rinella: page 88

Original Book Photography
Photographer John Lee
Photographer's Assistant Emily Simons
Food Stylist Lillian Kang
Food Stylist's Assistant Alexa Hyman

Chapter Opener Illustrations Eight Hour Day

Photography by Travis Rathbone: Cover, 19, 20, 23, 31, 32, 46, 72,
93, 94, 98, 149, 160, 195, 197; John Lee: 38–39, 59, 63, 84–85,
139, 145, 146–147, 174, 178–179, 183, 211; Plamen Petkov: 24,
37, 43, 86, 116, 119, 120, 150, 155, 191, 207; Levi Brown: 53, 76,
82, 106, 115, 177, 202; Ted Morrisson: 40, 64, 131, 163, 169, 186;
Johnny Miller: 90, 102, 128, 164; Elizabeth Watt: 75, 81, 109; Denver
Bryan: 8–9, 28–29; Beth Galton: 101, 132; Bill Buckley: 68–69; Tom
Martineau: 79; Jens Mortensen: 142; Jonathan Miles: 13; Anthony
Licata: 11; Tim Romano: 136–137; Michael Sugrue: 4.

Field & Stream food styling by Roscoe Betsill.

Additional photography courtesy of Getty/Simon Bottomley: 14; Getty/
Greg Sweney: 112–113; Getty/David Olah: 15; Getty/ Joel Sartore: 156;
Dermot Conlan/PPSOP/Corbis: 124–125; Toshi Sasaki/amanaimages/
Corbis: 49; iStockPhoto: 144, 196, 224; Shutterstock: 51, 129, 167,
170–171, 176, 184–185, 192, 198, 205, 209, 212–213, 214, 215,
222; Juniors Bildarchiv GmbH/Alamy: 97; Whit Richardson/Alamy: 194;
Tosh Brown/Alamy: 220–221; GalleryStock: 2–3.

JONATHAN MILES has been *Field & Stream*'s Wild Chef columnist since 2004. The author of two novels, he is the former *New York Times* cocktails columnist as well as a contributor to *Food & Wine, Garden & Gun*, and many other magazines, and his writing has been selected numerous times for the *Best American Sports Writing* anthologies. An avid hunter and angler, he also competed in the 2005 Dakar Rally, a 6,000-mile off-road race from Barcelona, Spain to Dakar, Senegal. He lives with his family along the Delaware River in rural New Jersey.